FROM IMPOSSIBLE TO POSSIBLE

TWO SIMPLE RULES TO ASSURE EXCEPTIONAL PUBLIC VALUE

Andrew Hollo

First published in 2018 by Grammar Factory Pty Ltd.

A catalogue record for this
book is available from the
National Library of Australia

Printed in Australia by McPhersons Printing
Cover design by Charlotte Gelin Design
Book production and editorial services by Grammar Factory

Disclaimer

The material in this publication is of the nature of general comment only, and does not represent professional advice. It is not intended to provide specific guidance for particular circumstances and it should not be relied on as the basis for any decision to take action or not take action on any matter which it covers. Readers should obtain professional advice where appropriate, before making any such decision. To the maximum extent permitted by law, the author and publisher disclaim all responsibility and liability to any person, arising directly or indirectly from any person taking or not taking action based on the information in this publication.

Contents

For my son Jasper, whose generation will benefit from all we create today.

Foreword

Aristotle proclaimed, 'Give me a lever and I can move the world!' (If he didn't say that, he should have.) The metaphor for us, a couple of thousand years later, is about leverage.

Once upon a time, public schools, family dinner tables and religious institutions instilled morality, a work ethic, and a safety net for society in industrialised countries. In my country, the United States, government entered the picture in 1935 with Franklin Roosevelt's 'New Deal' and the advent of social security: a government-guaranteed safety net.

Yet social security was based on actuarial tables that showed fourteen people working for every one retired, and an average life expectancy of sixty-eight after retirement at sixty-five. Today, there are about two people working for every retired person, and the latter's life expectancy is now eighty. Thus, far fewer people supporting far longer lives doesn't work, in this country or in any other.

Similarly, the minimum wage was enacted in 1938 to help support people working part-time, or temporarily, as they sought more meaningful work. Yet today it is expected to support people with families as full-time work.

Our traditional institutions and beliefs have changed dramatically and we need leverage to effectively deal with them today. It's not the leverage of Aristotle forcing a huge rock off the path, but rather the leverage of combined minds and synergistic groups nudging us all onto the right road.

In this highly readable and fascinating book, Andrew Hollo moves analytically and methodically through steps that demonstrate how public policy and private interests can be combined to create profound change. If you're sceptical about that, let me remind you that (in the US) as I write this, traffic fatalities are at an all-time low, unemployment is virtually non-existent, minority unemployment is the lowest it's been since anyone started counting it five decades ago, and murders in New York City have gone down from over 2,000 in 1990 to 280 in 2017.

I use my experience here in the US, but wherever in the world you're reading this, you'll probably find similar trends. That's because public and private interests have indeed often come together to create positive change. Yet those joint efforts have too often been by accident, not design, and great potential is being wasted while great problems are allowed to grow bolder and older.

As I write this, Germany, the fourth largest economy in terms of GDP and twenty-eight per cent of the EU economy, has launched a ferociously expensive new destroyer which has no sonar and poor anti-aircraft defences; their new Berlin airport is ten years late; and their new Stuttgart train station is several years late and far over budget. I don't ascribe this to a lack of prowess, but rather to a lack of will that occurs when politicians, private sector companies and the public interests do not coincide, but rather collide.

Andrew Hollo, who has done profound work for these exact parties and disparate interests, is the only person I know in my thirty years of global consulting with complex public and private entities who has consistently created commonality of interest and strong will. Other consultants would walk away, afraid of the perceived morass. But Andrew has managed to go From Impossible to Possible.

To many, this book may seem like science fiction. But to those of us who have been in the trenches, we recognise the brilliance behind a completely coherent and bold approach to solving the major problems of our times. That's a major undertaking, and this is a major book.

Alan Weiss, PhD
Author, *Million Dollar Consulting, Million Dollar Maverick* and over sixty other books

Making the impossible possible

As a species, we humans are experts at making the impossible possible.

In just the last twenty years, we've halved the number of people in poverty globally (that's a billion fewer people in severe poverty). In Australia, we've made roads half as dangerous (that's saved 100,000 lives). In my home state of Victoria, we've got 90% of our kids to finish school (compared to 73% in the year 2000). [1]

These are just three areas where visionary people like you have made remarkable things happen, relatively quickly.

The first edition of this book was quickly sold out in 2018 and I had countless fascinating conversations with readers about their journey from making the impossible possible. All were working in quite different areas. One was making housing affordable in one of the world's most expensive cities (Sydney). Another has been making university education work for people with full-time, low-income jobs (in Melbourne). Another still is turning a cultural backwater (Hobart) into a world-renowned modern art attraction.

In the last year, what I've noticed is that they all had some common features:

- A fundamental insight that sparked their vision which often grew to the scale of an obsession

---

1   "Data Source - Education and Work (Survey Of)." Australian Bureau of Statistics, Australian Government. October 20, 2017. Accessed March 28, 2019. http://www.abs.gov.au/ausstats/abs@.nsf/dossbytitle/09F494FB1EA20EC8CA256BD00026A755?OpenDocument.

- A group of people (sometimes quite a small group) who were their grassroots, 'ground up' believers

- A willingness to disrupt old ways of doing things

- A clear picture of whom they had to influence — and confidence to handle predictable disbelief and criticism

- The ability to talk about goals and outcomes, not just activities and tasks

- A very real awareness that things will go wrong along the way — and a plan for dealing with these

All of this great work is happening in a world which is slowly moving away from traditional concepts that differentiated 'public' from 'private', or 'for profit' from 'not for profit'. It's no longer the sole job of non-profits or governments to create public value. In fact, we live in a world where people are increasingly cynical about public sector agencies, especially governments, many of which are perceived as inefficient and ineffectual, hidebound and stultified, overly complex and self-serving. This is because they have become ends unto themselves. They have unclear goals, and sometimes no goals at all. They get stuck doing the same thing they've always done. As a result, they fail to make an impact. They simply can't cut through the noise and become visible.

Where does the cynicism about the public sector come from? Is it because, over decades, we all have raised our expectations generally? Is it an increasing division in society between the haves (who enjoy all the World's Most Liveable City benefits) and the have-nots (who don't)? Is it ideological to criticise the public sector to which all taxpayers compulsorily contribute? Whatever the reasons, there are limits to the impact that public value organisations can achieve when we continue to use outdated welfare models from the twentieth century, and even more outdated charity models from the nineteenth.

To continue making progress, and to quieten the critics, we now need a different way of doing things. The next big change will come from organisations that consider themselves social investors, or social change agents. This boundary blurring occurs when 'not-for-profits' more accurately focus on becoming 'not-for-loss', and where businesses will develop profit models that come from performing socially valued roles. If you want to read more about how these investment models are emerging, download the white paper from the Workwell website workwell.com.au/resources/white-pages/impact-investor.

Many social investment organisations are invisible to the general public. But many are not. Some of the world's greatest contributors to public value are also its most visible. Think about household names such as Greenpeace, the National Geographic Society, World Vision, the Museum of Modern Art (MoMA), Amnesty International and UNICEF. While these organisations span environment, human rights, the arts and health, they are also highly sustainable: they have revenue streams, partnerships and public profiles that assure their continuity. But there are many, many other government agencies and non-profits with just as credible and respected brands, which are also sustainable. Examples include Médecins Sans Frontières (Doctors Without Borders), Kiva, Oxfam and, here in Australia, The Smith Family, Bendigo Bank (and its subsidiary Community Sector Banking) and the Fred Hollows Foundation.

How do I know? Because I work with government agencies and nonprofits every single day. And I have developed some simple ways to help them transform themselves – and continue to change people's lives.

Solving the world's problems with two simple rules

My lifelong fascination with the intersection between business and public value stems from my earliest experiences. My parents were post-war migrant refugees who came to Australia as a promised 'golden land'. A place where revolutions didn't happen, where water flowed out of the tap and electricity worked at the click of a switch, where people with jobs bought houses and put food on the table, and where they raised children who could do the same. This got me deeply interested in what makes people, groups and entire societies work well – and, in contrast, not work at all. But the strongest imprint for me remains my primary school years. I was a gangly, short-sighted kid with a slightly strange name ('No, my last name doesn't have a "w" at the end'), who lived in a middle-class Anglo-Australian suburb, but couldn't play footy or cricket. None of that bothered me. What did bother me was that I was the only kid without a dad. Everyone else at my Catholic school had one.

My father was killed by a car while crossing the road outside his workplace one afternoon. I was just three, and my mother was eight months pregnant with my little brother. As a child, I'd sometimes ask my mum, 'Why am I the only kid without a dad?' But I soon stopped that when I realised how much it upset my mother. By the time I reached adulthood, and trained in psychology, I was asking a very different question: Apart from human error, what else failed that day my father was killed? The answers to me were pretty obvious. In the late 1960s, we had poor street lighting, poor car designs, poor roads, few regulations around drink driving, and few penalties for under-age driving (the boy who killed my dad was an under-age driver, at just seventeen). This line of questioning got me tremendously interested in how humans working in groups gradually make the world a better place. In particular, I became interested in how governments and non-profits work and, by my thirties, I'd decided to make these sectors my life's work.

The question I now ask is: How do public value organisations make the impossible possible? What's the difference between an agency that's seen as highly relevant, operating as a sustainable business and achieving very high impact, and one that isn't?

What I've discovered is that many public value organisations face the same four problems, regardless of the sector they're in:

1. **Knowing their product, but not their value.** This occurs when organisations concentrate on being busy, but fail to measure outcomes or impact. In other words, they are good at measuring processes, but are not good at measuring results. So, the 'means' are easily understood (number of patient appointments booked, number of environmental offences logged, and so on), but not the 'ends' (improvements in health, a cleaner environment, and so on).

2. **Being invisible, unknown or even misunderstood.** This is a case of not enough people knowing how good they are. This can include their own staff, who don't know the full extent of their own agency's work, or their customers, who don't grasp the full value available to them. Most often, however, it relates to non-customers or potential customers, as well as supporters, funders, investors and partners, to whom the organisation is either invisible, irrelevant or, even worse, maligned.

3. **Making hard decisions about what to keep and what to let go of, and which opportunities to go for and which to decline.** Public value organisations are not generally starved of opportunities. Rather, there's a glut of opportunities. It is therefore hard to know what

to decline and what to invest in. Steve Jobs famously said, 'People think focus means saying yes to the thing you've got to focus on. But that's not what it means at all. It means saying no to the hundred other good ideas that there are.'[2]

4. **Doing the same things, the same ways.** They're invested in functions, processes, technology, paperwork and capabilities that haven't changed for five, ten, twenty years or sometimes longer. Sometimes, they're performed by people who haven't changed roles in years!

One of my clients is a health service provider that delivers about twenty-five types of services to a local community – everything from counselling to podiatry, from helping old people remain in their homes, to helping struggling single parents raise their kids. Several years ago, the organisation had plenty of passion and was very busy. But it had no strategy to speak of – no systems to measure and manage results. It was visible to its users, but invisible to the very community it was trying to serve. I was shocked to discover that it didn't even have a website (this was in 2013!). Over our first year of working together, we did many things to boost the organisation's profile and impact. We set broad strategic goals that showed exactly how the organisation contributes to the social fabric of its community, and then linked these to precise outcomes which all staff understood and all managers could measure. Over three years, the organisation found that more people knew about it, its clients were even happier with the results they were getting, and its margins grew (as did its assets – by almost fifty per cent). It won Health Service of the Year for its size of organisation in 2015 and again in 2016 – the first time an organisation had won twice in consecutive years.

2   Jobs made this comment at a developer conference in 1997 when he had just begun returning Apple from the brink of bankruptcy. Jobs shrank Apple's products from '350 crappy products' to fewer than ten 'incredibly designed products'.

In this book, you'll discover how this non-profit – and others like it – underwent such a massive transformation. You'll learn:

- How to clarify your identity by asking and answering five fundamental questions, especially when you're working in a complex and changing environment.

- How to set crystal clear goals which match your public mission, and work out ways to be accountable for these.

- How to make tough decisions, bring your biggest ideas to life, rapidly assess opportunities, and genuinely co-design with your customers.

This book is the sum of my work as a strategist and facilitator with thousands of people who deliver public value, many of whom have faced, and solved, the same pain points you yourself face. Most of them are in government and in non-profits, but many are also self-employed, in social enterprises and, increasingly, in for-profit businesses. In order to cut through the noise, and make a solid and lasting everyday impact, there are two rules you need to follow. Yes, just two:

> Rule 1: Know what your everyday impact should be.

> Rule 2: Create everyday impact, every day.

If these rules sound simple, that's because they are. I happen to agree with Warren Buffet, who famously said, 'It is not necessary to do extraordinary things to get extraordinary results.' Instead, you should focus on the right things, which make you relevant, and which enable you to compete for public value. Your competitive advantage can be found in small things, if you do them every day. Warren Buffet has attributed his success to doing 'above average work for a very long time, which compounds to create great success'.

In my twenty years of consulting, I have observed and researched hundreds of high-impact public value businesses. This book, which is split into two parts, is the distillation of those years. The diagram below illustrates the eleven key areas that the most successful organisations are clear on. Each chapter in this book tackles one of those areas.

Purpose
Why you are in business

Role
The service you provide and don't provide

Scale
The size of the impact you're trying to achieve

Goals
How you measure success

Values
The shared beliefs that make you special or unique

Leverage
How well you use your customers to amplify your efforts

Partner
How you ally with those who also serve your customers in ways you don't or can't

Focus
How well you do what matters the most and stop doing that which doesn't add value

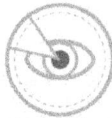

Future Proof
How well you do new things new ways rather than the old things old ways

Results
How well you ensure every effort leads to an outcome

Profile
How well you shamelessly build positive awareness of your work

In Part 1, I'll show you how to follow the first rule (know what your everyday impact should be) by helping you and your organisation determine your purpose, role, goals, values and scale. You'll do this by answering five key questions:

Chapter 1: Why do we exist? (This is your purpose.)

Chapter 2: What do we do? (This is your role.)

Chapter 3: How big can our impact be? (This is your scale.)

Chapter 4: How do we know we're successful? (These are your goals.)

Chapter 5: What makes us special? (These are your values.)

These five questions are followed by Chapter 6: Gaining Traction, which is where you will start turning knowledge into action.

Then in Part 2, I'll show you how to follow the second rule (create everyday impact, every day), by providing examples of best practice in some of the world's most successful public value organisations. There are six things to focus on here:

Chapter 7: Results. People own the outcomes they care most about.

Chapter 8: Focus. Prioritise your effort on what matters the most.

Chapter 9: Futureproof. Change things constantly and innovate, so tomorrow isn't the same as yesterday.

Chapter 10: Leverage. Do more with less by getting your customers to self-determine and self-manage.

Chapter 11: Partner. Find complementary organisations and people who can dramatically extend your value to your ideal customers.

Chapter 12: Profile. Tell stories and show your results, so you're seen the way you want to be.

To work out what your real impact can be in an increasingly competitive and market-driven environment, you don't need a large team of consultants camped out in your offices, doing analytical work and preparing impressive slide decks. Nor do you need to take teams of people away on numerous multi-day retreats. All you need are these two simple, yet powerful, rules.

In this book, you'll discover frameworks and strategic processes that I've developed over twenty years, which overcome all of the common hurdles that stop government agencies and non-profits from doing their best work. These processes work for any organisation delivering public value, especially where change pressure is strong, whether that pressure is economic, social or political.

If you're determined to make the impossible possible, let me show you how.

Andrew Hollo
Melbourne, April 2019

Part 1: Know what your everyday impact should be

The problem: In the twenty-first century, public value organisations cannot behave like charities or like professionalised bureaucracies. If they do, funders will not support them, and their constituents won't find them relevant. Instead, they must behave more and more like businesses, yet with a laser-sharp focus on their mission. But strategy is overcomplicated by an entire industry that exists to develop it. Organisations take far too long to form it, and far too little attention is paid to strategy internalisation (making sure everyone understands their part in it). Consequently, more than half of all CEOs say they have little confidence in their strategy.

The solution: Thriving in the world of impact investing requires discipline. That discipline is partly in the execution of your mission, but initially in its formation. As a C-level executive or senior operational leader, you should be able to clearly and consistently state five things:

1. Why you are in business.
2. What service you provide.

3.   Where the organisation is heading.

4.   How you measure success.

5.   What makes your organisation special or unique.

In chapters one to five, I'll show you how to determine and articulate all five of those things. Each chapter title is framed as a question to help you reflect on the content and generate discussions with your colleagues. Then in Chapter 6, I'll show you how to internalise your strategy, using the insights you've gained in the previous chapters. By the end of Part 1, you and your team should have what it takes to reach a very clear agreement on the everyday impact you are seeking to create.

CHAPTER 1:

What is your purpose?

ANDREW'S OBSERVATION: About half of all non-profits and government agencies don't have a clear value proposition that describes their
ultimate 'prize' or benefit. They know their product, but not their value.

If you don't know your value, you'll struggle to make a long-lasting impact. After all, why should customers care about your organisation if
even you, or your frontline staff, are not 100 per cent sure what makes it
relevant and even irreplaceable to your customers?

It is no coincidence that the most sustainable public value organisations
are those which can define their purpose within a very clear niche. In
this chapter, I'll show you how to define your 'raison d'être' (the most
important reason or purpose for your existence), and explain the significance of the 'aha' moment.

Defining your raison d'être

Can you name half-a-dozen businesses or organisations that you'd care
about if they disappeared tomorrow? Apart from the obvious ones (like
utility or energy companies), whose presence would you miss on a day-
to-day basis? My list would look something like this:

1. **Apple.** This company pretty much runs my business for me, from a
   hardware, software and data-storage perspective.

2. **Archie's All Day and The Kettle Black.** These are two local cafes (one
   near my office, the other near my son's school), where the staff know me
   by name. Each is a place where I can think, work, and even meet clients.

3. **5th Element Wellness.** This is where I do twice-weekly personal training sessions, occasional yoga classes, and sweat in the sauna. Without these few hours, I'd feel lethargic, unfocused and unhealthy.

4. **Qantas.** I advise organisations all around Australia, and have colleagues and peers all around the world, which means I spend a lot of time travelling. A good, solid airline, which is safe and reliable, is gold in my view.

5. **Queen Victoria Market.** A Melbourne institution, which my family and I treat as our local supermarket.

6. **Amazon.** I still remember the first time I ordered a book from Amazon. I put in my credit card details and my shipping address, and they promised delivery within a week. It arrived in three days, for a third less than what I would have paid at my local bookshop. To this day, I continue to buy books, video content and stationery from them.

Which businesses are on your list? And why did they make it there? Most of mine are about ease and convenience (Apple, Qantas, Amazon) and the quality of the experience (Apple, QVM, 5EW). While Apple, 5EW and QVM certainly have competitors, they offer a distinctive (and they'd argue unique) value proposition that is irreplaceable. There is a secret sauce, a raison d'être, a complex assembly of capabilities that represents a very high barrier to entry for other businesses.

How is this created and captured? The best public value organisations, like the best brands, do this superbly. How? By developing and implementing a clearly defined strategy. Some of my clients misunderstand strategy – they think it's a plan. Others think it's a list of prioritised actions. Still others believe strategy is a marketing slogan or tagline. In reality, it's none of these. Instead, this is what I tell my clients: Strategy is a collection of insights that compellingly explain why you do what you do, and for whom, and that provides a framework for decisions to be made.

The starting point for all strategic insights is being able to articulate a single business objective. If we were Amazon executives, for example, we might say something like, 'We are in business to be the dominant online retailer in a variety of product categories.' Or, if we were being extremely candid, we might even say, 'We are in business to eliminate bricks-and-mortar retailing.' If someone asked, 'What's wrong with bricks-and-mortar retailers?', Amazon could identify a number of problems, including:

1. **Lack of choice.** When I shop at a physical store, I am limited to what makes economic and logistical sense for the retailer to stock, which means stock is always limited.

2. **Lack of convenience.** When I shop at a physical store, I have to locate it, travel there, find my way around the store, ask for help if I'm confused, queue up, pay, and travel home. There are many steps involved.

3. **Uncompetitive prices.** When I shop at a physical store, I pay a price that factors in the cost of the store's overheads, including rent, staff, and so on. This means I pay more than I need to.

Think for a moment about your own organisation. Can you clearly articulate an overarching goal or objective? To do this, think about who your ideal customer or beneficiary is. Amazon's is very broad – literally any consumer with internet access. The World Wildlife Fund's beneficiaries are animals living in threatened wilderness areas. Doctors Without Borders' customers are sick and injured people in war zones. Who are yours?

Once you have an ideal customer in your sights, ask: What is the biggest problem they need solved? Amazon recognised very early that our reliance on bricks-and-mortar stores creates problems of availability, value and ease. Doctors Without Borders realised that war zones, or epidemics, create demand for First World healthcare, precisely at times and in places when it's unlikely to be found. WWF helps solve problems of human encroachment on migratory patterns, problems of climate change on ecological systems, and problems of economic development on species' habitats. What are the problems that your ideal customer wants solved?

Finally, you can distil these problems into a single purpose statement, or raison d'être. Doctors Without Borders' purpose statement is: 'To help people anywhere in the world who can't get healthcare and where need is greatest, because of conflict, disasters or epidemics.' WWF's purpose statement is: 'To stop the degradation of the planet's natural environment and to build a future in which humans live in harmony with nature'. Use the smallest number of words to come up with your own purpose statement, without resorting to generic or 'motherhood' statements.

If this isn't obvious to you, or you get tangled up in large numbers of problems, it might be worth waiting for an 'aha' moment.

The 'aha' moment

Every single successful enterprise that delivers public value, be it for-profit or non-profit, can be tracked back to some sort of 'aha' moment. In the late 1960s, the US deregulated its airline industry on a state basis. Jets and fuel were becoming significantly cheaper, and people were becoming more mobile. A Texan lawyer named Herb Kelleher had an 'aha' moment: A short-haul flight should be as cheap as driving. And just like that, Southwest Airlines was born. In Kelleher's words, 'We're not competing with other airlines. We're competing with ground transportation.' Southwest Airlines is now the world's largest and most profitable low-cost carrier, offering more than 3,000 flights per day, with the purpose of 'connecting people to what's important in their lives through friendly, reliable, and low-cost air travel'.

While Amazon and Southwest Airlines offer private, not public, value, they have a clear purpose because they solve recognised, and long-in-tractable, problems. Let's look at a non-profit example, to make my case applicable to every type of organisation.

In 2008, two Australian university students, Daniel Flynn and his then girl-friend Justine (who is now his wife), and another friend, Jarryd, watched a documentary about the lack of clean water in disadvantaged countries. Specifically, how 600 million people simply can't get daily access to reliable, clean water. Yet in Australia alone, people spend $600 million a year on bot-tled water – even though the tap water is perfectly safe to drink. This insight led to a profound 'aha' moment: What if we could turn bottled water for those who don't need it into clean water for those who really do need it? This led to the creation of the social enterprise Thankyou, which has a clear pur-pose: 'By the simple act of buying a bottle of water, every Australian can be a micro-philanthropist.' Or, to put it another way: 'Empowering humanity to choose a world without poverty.' In addition to water, the business now sells cereals and snack bars, body care products and baby products. All profits are given to those in need. To date, Thankyou has helped 150,000 people access clean water, and 190,000 people access hygiene and sanitation.

If, like Southwest Airlines and Thankyou Water, your purpose state-ment stems from some sort of 'aha' moment, it's important to remember that a purpose statement is beneficial because it is unambiguous. Most organisations operate in complex environments where many decisions have to be made routinely. Therefore, any 'hack' or heuristic that aids quick decision making, and reduces what is called cognitive load[3], has tremendous value. When Southwest Airlines staff would propose in-flight options such as video-on-demand services or meal services, Herb Kelleher would always ask the same question: 'How does that help us to be affordable?' Or when engineering staff proposed more diverse types of planes, he'd ask: 'How does that help us to be more reliable?'

The best purpose statements achieve three things:

- They are specific to the organisation, and aren't interchangeable with those of others.
- The problems claimed to be solved strongly resonate with customers.
- They can be used as yes-no shortcuts for high-level decision making.

Frequently asked questions

My clients typically ask five questions about creating purpose statements. I've listed them here, along with my answers.

1. **'We are a provider of quality, accessible healthcare services'. Is this a purpose statement?**

   The answer is no. This statement answers a different question (what's your role), which we'll look at in the next chapter. To turn 'We are a provider of X' into a purpose statement, you have to ask why you are a provider of X. What problems are solved by providing X? Or, if you took away X, what would be missing from people's lives?

   My advice to this particular client was to clarify what sort of people are specifically looking for quality, accessible healthcare services, and

---

3   Cognitive load refers to the total amount of mental effort being used in a person's working memory at any given time.

why. Approaching the exercise in this way led to the following purpose statement: 'We exist so that families and children enjoy the best health possible, at an affordable cost.' This speaks to the problems they solve for families – quality, access and cost of primary healthcare.

2. **What if our purpose is very generic? For instance: 'We exist so that young people live positive and engaged lives.'**

   This statement could apply to an educational institution, a post-prison release program, a mental health online peer support network, or even a relationship advice centre for teenagers. There is nothing wrong with having a generic purpose statement, as it's quite probable that educators, prison programs, counselling programs and the like are all directed towards the same higher end-goal or, in other words, helping solve the same types of problems. This is no issue as long as you can speak to the problem statement inherent in your purpose. In this case, as long as you can answer the question: 'Which young people specifically are unengaged, or negative, and why?', you can work with a generic purpose statement. Remember also that a good purpose statement is a heuristic for decisions, so any venture you enter into should answer the question: How would this help young people live positive and engaged lives?

3. **Is it okay to change our purpose?**

   Your purpose should be the most durable part of your strategy. Amazon's purpose of dominating online retailing has been consistent for over twenty years, while Southwest Airlines' purpose has been very similar for forty. Having said that, the circumstances in which you operate could change, and there are numerous instances of re-evaluations of purpose.

   Take the King's Fund in the UK, which was set up in the 1890s during the reign of Queen Victoria. Its initial purpose was to contribute funding to London's voluntary hospitals, before extending its operations to the inspection of hospitals, and creating a system to efficiently distribute health services to address the growth of the city. Then, when the tax-funded National Health Service was established in 1948, the King's Fund evolved into a think tank. You should think about change in purpose when one of the following has, or will, occur:

- Your ideal customer is changing (like the King's Fund).

- Your ideal customer's 'old problems' have been largely solved, but they have new problems.

- You are changing scope and need a broader purpose (like Thankyou did when it moved from just bottled water into cleaning, body care and baby products).

4. **Why is it called a purpose statement rather than a vision statement or a mission statement?**

In my experience, only half of all organisations that use these terms use them correctly. Vision describes 'ends', while mission describes 'means'. As an example, Mahatma Gandhi's *vision* was Indian independence from British rule. His *mission* was non-violent, passive resistance. The vision describes *why* Gandhi led the independence movement (to free India from British rule) while the other describes *how* he did it (by facing down British colonists with stirring speeches and non-violent protest). I find people are confused by this distinction, and therefore I much prefer talking about your purpose (why you exist) and then, separately, your role (what you do). The former can be aspirational, even lofty and idealistic, whereas the latter must be grounded firmly in capability and capacity (we'll discuss this in more detail in the next chapter).

5. Should we specify who benefits from our purpose?

'Not always' is the simple answer. While a purpose should indicate problems solved, it is possible that your purpose statement may imply a large number of beneficiaries. Consider NASA's purpose statement: 'Reveal the unknown for the benefit of humankind.' Who benefits from human space survival? Who benefits from lunar landings? Who benefits from humans living in and returning from space? And who benefits from a deeper understanding of the universe? The answer is simple: All of us. NASA's early work on launch vehicles, communication satellites and weather satellites has fundamentally changed daily life and created whole new industries. As a catalyst for international cooperation, NASA has also changed how and why humanity conducts space exploration. Now, NASA is preparing to take mankind farther than ever before as it helps to foster a robust commercial space economy near Earth, and pioneers further human and robotic exploration on the journey to Mars.

There is no single answer to this question. Depending on your scale, you may imply broad beneficiaries (all of humanity, like NASA, or all endangered wildlife, like WWF), state somewhat specific beneficiaries (like children and families in a particular region who want the best possible health, or young people who are disengaged from school), or clearly articulate a strong niche (such as women who have experienced domestic violence and are seeking to enter the workforce). Just remember that if you specify a niche, you may need to re-evaluate your purpose more frequently, as its use as a decision-making shortcut will be tested more often.

ACTION TO TAKE

Clarity of purpose is paramount to gaining support from investors and funders, attracting and recruiting the right people, and keeping your people and resources focused on the job.

If you already have a purpose statement, do a 'desktop test' of it by asking:

1. Does it state or imply our ideal target audience?

2. Does it imply their biggest problems, which we help solve?

3. How does it help us make decisions?

If you don't already have a purpose statement that you are happy with, then start with 'aha' moments and complete the following sentences:

1. Three big insights about the world we live in are _____, _____ and _____.

2. The problems we solve are _____.

3. We exist so that _____.

If you don't have answers to these, or your answers are vague and imprecise, don't worry. Keep reading and, by the end of Part 1, you'll have some pointers for vital conversations you can have with your colleagues and customers.

CHAPTER 2:

What is your role?

ANDREW'S OBSERVATION: The problem isn't that public value organ-isations don't do enough. On the contrary, there are too many non-profits and government agencies that do too many things. They offer 'all things to all people' and therefore end up giving too few things to too few people.

In the last chapter, we looked at public value organisations (and for-prof-it businesses) that have tremendously clear purpose, grounded in clarity about the types of problems they're solving, which helps guide decisions about what they should and shouldn't do. An organisation's role tells us what they do that leads the beneficiary to the organisation's purpose. If Amazon's purpose is to dominate online retailing because it has a solu-tion to problems of choice, convenience and cost, *what is that solution?* In other words, *what does Amazon actually do?*

This is where Amazon becomes *a fulfilment company,* or Thankyou becomes *a marketing and distribution company.* In other words, the ideal role of a highly competitive organisation is to offer a complete and remarkable solution to problems recognisable to the customer. For Amazon to be complete and remarkable, it needed to surmount one advantage that bricks-and-mortar retail offers over online retailing: Im-mediate use. I can walk out of a stationery store with my whiteboard markers and start using them immediately. Therefore, Amazon speci-fied that its role becomes not just the fulfilment of online orders, but *the same-day (or next day) fulfilment of online orders.* That conditional is terribly important, because it becomes the pivot point for capability and capacity-building in that company.

Later on, in Chapter 8, I'll look at how you set priorities. (In Amazon's case, all priorities must lead back to this pivot point. In other words, the company invests in those initiatives which enable the same-day fulfilment of online orders.) But before you do that, you must be crystal clear on the role of your organisation. Clear specification of role is vital because it allows you to differentiate yourself from competitors and find the right positioning in increasingly contested markets (Thankyou is one of many bottled water suppliers, but its highly targeted marketing makes it the only social-value bottled water company). It ensures you build the right capabilities in line with your service offerings (Thankyou needs to build branding and distribution capabilities first and foremost). And it makes sure you can prove your results (Thankyou's reach and uptake, and ultimately its sales and contributions to water projects, are directly linked to its effectiveness in marketing and distribution). In this chapter, I'll show you how to gain clarity about your organisation's role.

Gaining clarity

We don't need to search far to find examples of clear and clever thinking about role in investor impact businesses. Just this morning, I caught a lift in an office building where the digital display advertisements showed graphic before-and-after footage of Nepali children with eye diseases. The Fred Hollows Foundation was formed after the death of its namesake, an ophthalmologist who worked extensively in indigenous communities where preventable eye diseases, such as trachoma, are rife. Fred Hollows' purpose was crystal clear: People should not end up blind for life because proper medical treatment is unreachable where they live.

The foundation has sensibly limited itself to just one role: Building capacity. Specifically, putting capable people plus capable technology, especially lowest cost, distributable technology, where it doesn't already exist. The 'aha' moment for Fred Hollows was that people and technology needn't cost the sort of money that we in developed countries pay for such treatment. The foundation therefore trains medical staff to be able to accurately diagnose and treat eye conditions. Building a local health force was always considered the best way to ensure the foundation would have a lasting impact. That includes not only training doctors, nurses, surgeons, and so on, but also community health workers – people who are trained to recognise dangerous eye diseases and who can refer patients to qualified doctors.

In the 1980s, a small organisation called the Health Issues Centre was formed with the goal of giving health consumers a voice in their healthcare. In a recent speech, HIC's chief executive, Danny Vadasz, quoted the anthropologist Margaret Mead: 'Never doubt that a small group of thoughtful, committed citizens can change the world. Indeed, it is the only thing that ever has.' This fundamental premise hasn't changed. But in almost forty years, HIC's role has changed a lot. Much of its original business was training consumer advocates; people who speak as 'voice of the consumer' on public hospital boards, advisory committees, and so on. However, we now live in a world where the right for consumer representation doesn't have to be fought for (it's now legislated and regulated), yet we also live in a world where more active consumers – who are unhappy with their medical information, options and treatment – are not taking to the streets or picketing medical clinics, but are taking to social media. This is where Danny sees the next big wave of change. Therefore, when we worked together, his board reviewed its role for the next phase of work and narrowed its focus to just three things:

GIVE A VOICE

HIC wants many more voices to be heard, not just the usual voices (those largely grey-haired consumer representatives who have ample time – and skills – to volunteer on hospital advisory committees). Giving a voice therefore becomes much more than just training people on how to contribute to these committees. It becomes more about how to train them to be vocal, powerful agitators. It also means changing the very meaning of what engagement means. Danny's team built an art installation which invited viewers to think about what would happen to them as they aged and got closer to the end of their lives. Such emotionally powerful experiences mean that participants are more likely to speak up and voice an opinion about their own care.

SHINE A SPOTLIGHT

HIC realises that it needs to make visible the impacts of health issues on real people. In other words, there is a problem around how health issues, especially hidden health issues, are revealed. HIC's role here is twofold: To use social media campaigns to shine the spotlight into dark corners, and to operate an 'adverse outcomes register' on behalf of government, so that the spotlight stays switched on.

RATTLE CAGES

There are many 'owners' of the health system: Governments, funders, investors, operators, regulators, professional bodies, educators, and more. All are ultimately well intentioned, but they also hold on to their power tightly. HIC aims to challenge mindsets and practices through making recommendations, largely to healthcare deliverers but also to professional associations and policy makers. It can do this only if it's perceived as impartial and independent, in full command of the facts, and having trusting relationships with health system 'owners'.

Why these three? Because they were judged as the most powerful levers by which to achieve the purpose of HIC. In essence, they create a value chain for HIC, an idea which I'll explain further in Chapter 7. Note how the roles are complementary, not just additional. In other words, rattling cages builds on evidence gained from shining spotlights, while both are based upon a premise that a vocal health consumer will be one who's unafraid to speak when the spotlight is shone their way. These three roles also become a virtuous circle. Meaning, when cages are successfully rattled, practices change and people who are informed about this believe in the efficacy of speaking up. This reinforces the likelihood that they will speak up, because they see a reasonable prospect of change in doing so.

The most important point to make here is that you should specify a role (or roles) that enables achievement of purpose most quickly, effectively and efficiently. Both Fred Hollows and Amazon do this very well. The second most important feature about role is that it should be based on what you're very, very good at. A useful exercise I carry out with some of my clients is to ask three questions:

1. What do you do that you are *unique* at? In other words, what could you speak about at a conference, to a rapt audience, willing to learn from you? The Fred Hollows Foundation (FHF) is uniquely skilled at doorstep diagnoses. In other words, identifying and training community health workers to recognise dangerous eye diseases, and then refer patients to FHF doctors.

2. What do you do that you are *distinctive* at? In other words, what sets you apart? It may be a way of delivering service, a target demographic unserved by others, or the look and feel of a product. FHF is distinctive, but not unique, in its support for low-cost, high-tech inventions that further the organisation's purpose, such as the Arclight. This is a lightweight, portable and solar-powered ophthalmoscope, which is used to diagnose eye diseases and costs about ten dollars. Because of its affordability, it is the ideal tool to diagnose eye conditions in the developing world.

3. What do you do that you're merely *competitive* at? This is everything else. You shouldn't aim to be distinctive, let alone unique, at everything! That's a recipe for disaster. Pick one or two points of uniqueness, and one or two distinctive features, and make sure every other aspect of role is competitive. FHF is competitive in its training of doctors. There is no case to be made for the foundation stating that its doctors' training is better than what is on offer elsewhere, but there *is* an important case for stating that it is no worse than what you would find in any First World city.

Frequently asked questions

Here are three questions that my clients typically ask when they're grappling with how to delineate their role (along with my answers).

1. **Should we specify what we don't do?**

   Yes, sometimes that's valuable. For instance, it is important for a primary health network to specify that its role is facilitation and enablement of a primary healthcare ecosystem at a local level, but that its role is *not* to deliver health services. This enables it to take up opportunities as coordinators, capacity builders and system improvers, and clearly differentiates it from its partners and stakeholders, who are the deliverers. This also helps ease any potential competitive tensions.

2. **What if we're already doing too much?**

   I worked with a community health organisation that had forty-seven distinct service businesses. The two largest had revenues of over $8 million, while the smallest turned over just $30,000. We plotted them in order of revenue, and we ended up with a classic 'long tail' graph.

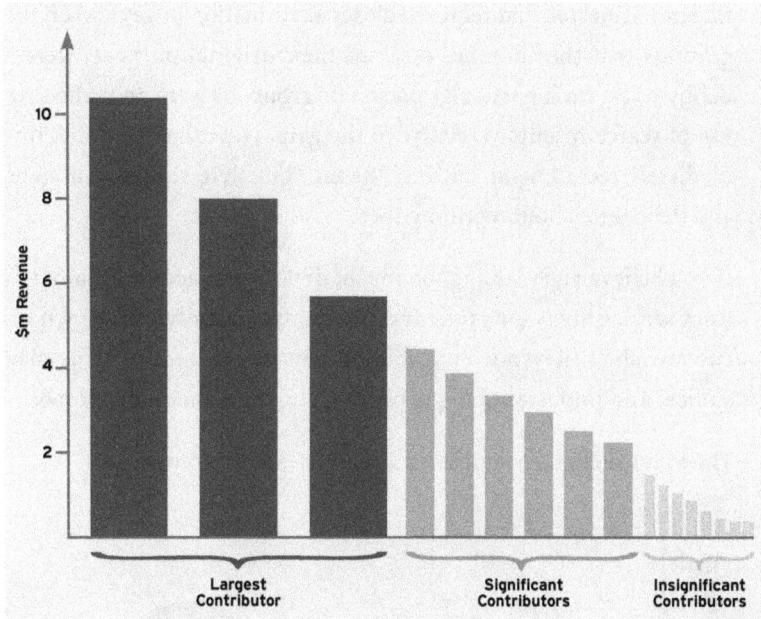

We divided these into three blocks. The first block encompassed the first three service areas, which comprised more than fifty per cent of the organisation's revenue. We asked a simple question: How closely related are these primary businesses to our single purpose? (In one case, my client answered, 'The third one isn't', and we started making plans for exiting that business.) Next, we drew a block around the middle half dozen or so, which represented about thirty-five per cent of the organisation's revenue. We asked a different question here: Are we *competitive*, *distinctive* or *outstanding*? What can we do to move from one to the next? Last, we drew another box around the 'tail': Thirty-three businesses representing just fifteen per cent of total revenues.

We asked ourselves *both* of the prior questions, plus a third: Are we at least breaking even on each one of these? That yielded a total of fifteen businesses that required closer examination or review, on the grounds that they'd either outlived their original purpose, were a hobby horse for a particular person or group, or were an ineffective use of scarce resources relative to the gain. Note that we didn't immediately recommend 'cutting' the tail, but were simply conscious and deliberate about retaining these.

If you believe you're doing too much, divide your activities into distinct service areas (or profit and loss centres, ideally). Rate each on two variables: Revenue contribution (small, medium or large may suffice) and importance to purpose (again, high, medium or low).

Then plot them on a simple 2 x 2 matrix, like this one.

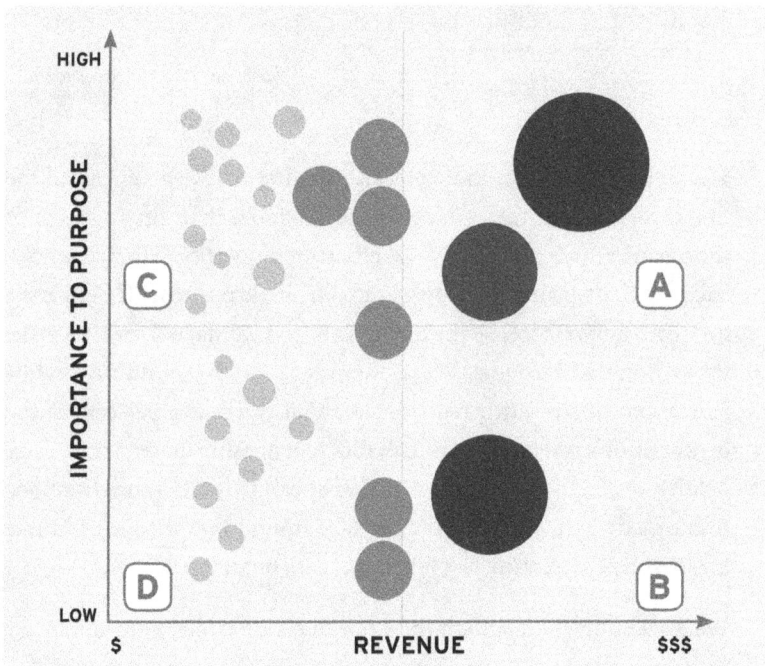

The upper right quadrant (A) is your essence – what you must protect, and expand if possible. The lower right quadrant (B) is where your cash cows live, so ask yourself if those revenue centres also generate significant margins. If not, improve margins, or exit.

The upper left quadrant (C) is for important business at smaller scale, so the analysis here should be: 'Can we build any of these and move them to (A)?' or, 'Can they contribute margins and stay in (C)?' Finally, you should seriously assess letting go of those in the lower left quadrant (D). They contribute neither revenues, nor purpose, and are often a distraction to a finely honed role.

3. **Can we change roles, or scope of services, over time?**

Yes. With some of my clients, I advocate 'amputating and re-growing', much as a lizard will lose its tail under times of threat, but is then capable of re-growing it as it nourishes itself. One of my clients struggled with business in the youth justice area until we agreed they should divest. They had qualms about losing this capability, but when I pointed out to them that they'd only lose the operations themselves, *not the ability to operate these services*, they were comfortable with the decision. Four years later, when different funding conditions prevailed, they were well positioned to bid for a multi-million-dollar program of work. You will know if your overall scope should change simply based on revenue contribution of your service areas. One of my clients was originally a hospital that operated inpatient services. It then moved to a mix of bed-based and community-based services, and finally was delivering eighty-five per cent of its services in the community, in patient's homes.

ACTION TO TAKE

Clearly defining your role means you can unambiguously state what you can uniquely deliver. Be ruthless - don't cling to old definitions of what you are if your revenue sources have moved on, or your service locations have changed. You'll know if you can state your role sufficiently when you and your team can complete these statements, preferably in language that makes sense to your customers:

1. We are uniquely, or distinctively, equipped to do _____.

2. Our competitors are _____. We are better than them because _____.

3. In order to offer a more remarkable and complete solution that addresses our purpose, we could be doing more in the area of _____.

4. To sharpen our focus, we could question or re-examine our current role of _____.

Completing the first two statements will help you know where to invest in capability, while completing the third and fourth statements will help you plan immediate or future improvements.

CHAPTER 3:

What is your scale?

ANDREW'S OBSERVATION: Many public value organisations stay stuck at a particular size. These organisations believe in their work, but they don't know how to build their business so as many people as possible benefit. Or, they're fearful that growth will dilute what makes them special. They are operating within a 'zone of certainty' around which their capabilities are designed.

Many of the entrepreneurially focused non-profits we examine in this book have begun almost as start-ups, using minimum viable products to test market acceptance. (A minimum viable product, or MVP, is a product with just enough features to satisfy early adopters, and to provide real market-sourced feedback for future service development.) Once that's done, they ask themselves, and their supporters, funders and investors, this question: How many people could benefit from this offer? In other words, what is the potential scale?

In this chapter, I'll reveal how to find the right scale for maximum impact and minimum risk, by focusing on two key factors: Purpose and capability. I'll also address the question of when a merger should (and shouldn't) become a way for you to build scale.

Letting your purpose drive your scale

Nancy Lublin's Dress for Success story is a remarkable case of purpose driving scale. In 1997, Nancy, then a second-year law student, received a $5,000 inheritance from her great-grandfather. She didn't know how to make this windfall gift into a sustainable project, so she found partners who did (three nuns!) and started Dress for Success. Originally, she offered a 'suiting service' for women attending job interviews who didn't own appropriate corporate clothing. A woman simply visited a Dress for Success boutique, where the volunteers helped her pick an interview outfit from the clothes that were donated. Aside from this, DFS provided guidance and coaching for the upcoming interview.

For many years, this model worked just fine, but Nancy realised that there were many missing ingredients. Believing that purpose drives scale, Nancy decided to add other core services. She opened career centres for women who wanted professional development, guidance and career opportunities. She also started helping women with career advancement goals through teaching financial literacy, leadership and civic participation. Nancy also partnered with numerous affiliates, enterprises and donors (more on this in Chapter 10).

The scaling method Nancy uses resembles a franchise model. Women who want to establish a Dress for Success organisation in their local area can apply to become an affiliate. Each affiliate is a community-based non-profit that helps women in their local area, and addresses particular challenges in their location. Each affiliate establishes and conducts its own fundraising efforts, programs, referral agency relationships, and manages its own volunteers. This method has allowed rapid, and successful, scaling. Nancy started with $5,000 and three New York City nuns, and now helps over one million women in 150 cities and twenty-seven countries, with continued growth planned.

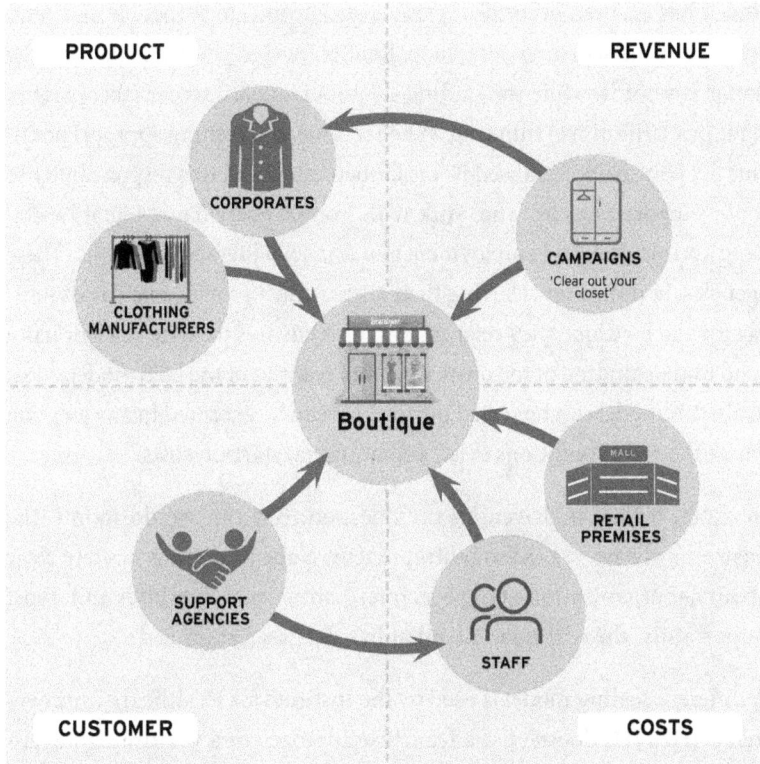

PRODUCT

REVENUE

CORPORATES

CLOTHING
MANUFACTURERS

CAMPAIGNS
'Clear out your
closet'

Boutique

RETAIL
PREMISES

SUPPORT
AGENCIES

STAFF

CUSTOMER

COSTS

This diagram shows how a self-sustaining loop is constructed around the core of the business, which is the boutique. This is where products (business attire) are 'sold' and services (support and education) are delivered. The revenue for the business is not from sale of garments, but from supporters (corporate organisations) who undertake campaigns (such as Clean Out Your Closet) that both raise money and collect donated business attire in good condition. This is added to clothing donated by fashion labels and manufacturers.

Nancy has ensured even the biggest costs beyond stock (people and rent) are part of the self-sustaining loop. Rent is covered wholly or partially by donor landlords, while the staffing solution truly is a remarkable piece of right-brain (intuitive) thinking. When it came to screening appropriate clients for DFS, Nancy realised it was far better to hand this responsibility to those support agencies who work with women every day: Mental health, drug and alcohol, and employment and financial literacy programs. These agencies, in return for referring their clients, must provide one day of staffing for the boutique they refer to. This also ensures that the referrer has a solid understanding of the on-the-ground realities of the DFS model. Most of all, this model can be scaled infinitely. It can be executed in any location where the right conditions exist, with minimal start-up costs.

In short, Nancy is driven by the question: But can we do more? The answer is always yes. As an entrepreneur, Nancy Lublin is acutely clear about her organisation's purpose, role, distinctive capabilities and, most importantly, the scaling model that has the greatest impact.

A different scaling model is used by the Institute for Healthcare Improvement (IHI). IHI doesn't use a franchise approach or a venture capital approach, but a campaign approach. In other words, what many organisations would call a strategic priority or key project, IHI calls a campaign, for which it enlists support. Consequently, its indicator of scale is not dollars (some $50 million in revenues) or locations, but the number of organisations and people engaged. IHI's scaling story spans over twenty-five years, in which time it has engaged almost one million health professionals per year, while almost 10,000 attend IHI's annual forum.

The key is to ensure your scaling model is appropriate for your purpose and role:

FROM IMPOSSIBLE TO POSSIBLE

- *If your purpose is large-scale behaviour change* (as is the case with IHI), then campaigns that can be scaled to reach large numbers of engaged people are perfect.

- *If your purpose is assertively reaching out and improving social outcomes* for marginalised and disempowered individuals (as is the case with DFS), then scaling up your number of local affiliates is perfect.

- *If your purpose is capitalising low-return business ventures* to build prosperity in developing nations, then a venture capital model, like Kiva's, is perfect.

There is consequently no one right way to scale; it all depends on your purpose:

- *If you're a service deliverer* (disability, health, aged care, and so on), greater scale comes about through cost-effective capability that allows you to *compete*.

- *If you're a research institute*, then your scaling strategy might be through partnerships (which we'll discuss in Part 2), which allow you to *differentiate*.

- *If you're a regulator or statutory body*, then your scaling strategy is through a transfer of responsibility based on risk (in other words, encouraging more self-regulation, and reserving your closest scrutiny for those most likely to cause harm), allowing you to achieve *greater reach*.

Determining scale based on capability

One of the main reasons that organisations remain within a zone of certainty relates to their capability. Boards and executives that are capable of running a single-site operation – with, say, forty staff and $5 million of revenues – are not necessarily going to be comfortable running a ten-site operation with 400 staff and $50 million of revenues, let alone a 100-site operation with 4,000 staff and half-a-billion dollars of revenues. Putting aside the question of purpose, let's ask ourselves why we can't jump orders of magnitude (tenfold leaps), except in rare instances. One past client who has done this is EACH (Eastern Access Community Health). In the 1980s, EACH was a suburban community health service, with a couple of sites from which it delivered a range of health services with revenues of less than $10 million. Today, it is the largest of thirty similar organisations, with revenues approaching $100 million, 1,000 staff, and fifty sites in most Australian states.

While some of EACH's growth came from just a couple of mergers over some twenty years, most of its scaling was done by showing its ability to deliver high-quality services that funders could trust[4]. Furthermore, a closer look at EACH shows it has mastered seven capabilities that I recommend to all public value service providers. Like in baseball, these can be thought of as 'bases' to reach. They apply to any organisation delivering any type of direct social service in a competitive market system, be it disability, aged care, community health, allied health, family violence, child protection, criminal justice and youth justice, early childhood, education or employment.

---

4   A term that program funders often use, colloquially, is 'A safe pair of hands.' This exposes them to little risk, and scale allows them to show desired impact while disbursing a high percentage of their funds in a timely way.

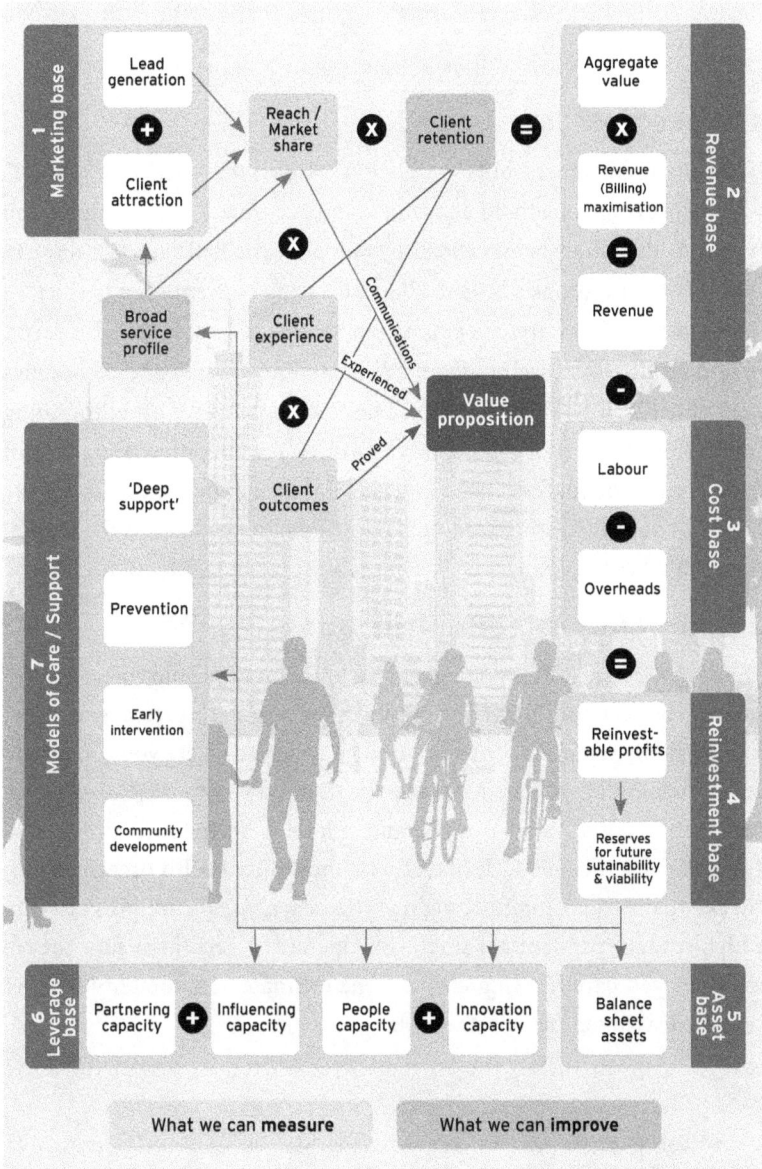

Marketing base — 1

- Lead generation
- Client attraction

Reach / Market share ⊗ Client retention =

Broad service profile

Client experience

Value proposition

'Deep support'

Prevention

Early intervention

Community development

Models of Care / Support — 7

Client outcomes

Communications

Experienced

Proved

Revenue base — 2

- Aggregate value ⊗
- Revenue (Billing) maximisation =
- Revenue

Cost base — 3

- Labour −
- Overheads =

Reinvestment base — 4

- Reinvestable profits
- Reserves for future sutainability & viability

Leverage base — 6

Partnering capacity ⊕ Influencing capacity

People capacity ⊕ Innovation capacity

Balance sheet assets

Asset base — 5

What we can **measure**   What we can **improve**

Put very simply, these are the seven things that any growth-oriented organisation needs to do:

GET CUSTOMERS

Not just any customers, but the right ones. This is the marketing base (#1) which ensures people hold a strong – and accurate – perception of you (your profile), which brings clients to your door (we'll discuss this more in Part 2). Organisations like EACH do this using conventional marketing methods to build awareness among their ideal customers, but also invest in building awareness among referrers (similar to DFS) and sometimes even 'own' the inbound referral systems for a region. This brand-building is often foreign territory to public value organisations attempting to shift from charity or professional models to investor models, especially the notion of actively testing who they reach, what percentage of the market they can take, and then assertively maximising client retention.

BRING MONEY THROUGH THE DOOR

The revenue base (#2) is made up of the number of people you can serve (more is better) multiplied by how much revenue each person generates, multiplied by retention. The best models are those where you can bill on some ongoing basis (like aged care or disability support), so you have revenue security. It's also important to look at ways to maximise revenue. For instance, EACH, like other community health organisations, checks that it is billing fully against Medicare. Aged care providers (of which seventy per cent are single-site operators) need to ensure they're making aged care funding claims. One estimate is that eighty-five per cent are leaving money on the table.[5]

---

5 'The Real Cost to Providers of Wrongful ACFI claims', Leading Age Services Australia, Fusion magazine, 2016

SPEND MONEY

On the right things. I could have said 'minimise spending', but this is the wrong message. You have to spend commensurate with your service offer. If you offer a niche service with highly specialised elements, you'll need to recruit the best people, who are expensive. Organisations like EACH will typically build a cost model that shows their fixed costs, and then how costs grow as scale grows. This enables them to work out how big they need to get to ensure each service is profitable.

DO SOMETHING VALUABLE WITH THE LEFTOVER MONEY

The difference between the revenue and cost bases, of course, is the reinvestment base (#4), which provides reserves to fund future growth, but also immediately re-investable profits.

BUILD ASSETS

Or at least don't deplete them to perilously low levels. Many non-profits have assets on their balance sheets that are poorly leveraged, in the form of property or even cash and other liquid assets, which they are not using effectively. One of my clients has recently identified a $20 million property that was fully paid off decades ago, yet they haven't considered what they could borrow against this to enable more services to be delivered.

INVEST IN YOURSELVES

This base involves spending money to amplify or leverage your desired impact. You choose to spend this money not on the delivery of services, but on making yourselves stronger and more capable. What you elect to spend money on will vary, but you should consider spending money on your people's capabilities (base level, but also specialist and leadership skills), influence (such as issues leadership and advocacy) and innovations (like data capability).

DELIVER THE BEST SERVICES POSSIBLE

This is spending money on the delivery of services, but also on the development of services people really want. Depending on your sector and your service suite, you may opt for deepening the support you provide, providing earlier interventions based on better detection and assessment, developing community capacity so that your services are required less acutely, or even removing root causes of the reasons people need your services in the first place.

In the middle of the diagram, of course, is the client, the customer. Your ultimate value proposition is made up of three things: (i) the outcomes you can demonstrably deliver (proof required!); (ii) the experience of the customer; and (iii) the numbers of customers that you reach.

Most of my clients want to use this diagram for diagnostic purposes. So, they want to know two things. First, what they can measure (in the diagram, these things are shaded in pale grey), and second, and more importantly, what they can change or improve (these are shaded in dark grey).

To merge or not to merge?

As a consultant, a very common request I have from client organisations that are moving into the impact investment space is whether they should merge to build scale, and how they should assess potential mergers. My simplest answers to them are 'Maybe' to the first question and 'Carefully' to the second. The truth is that I, along with other consultants, have provided strategic advice to a number of organisations undertaking the due diligence phases of mergers, or who have come out of that phase having decided not to merge. The process itself is hugely time-consuming and exhausting, and often leaves an organisation battle scarred and tentative about future merger or acquisition activity.

Also, it's important to note that some seventy per cent of mergers don't achieve their initially stated objectives[6].

So, a less flippant answer to the question is: 'You should merge when each entity's fundamental *purpose* is best served by doing so jointly.' In my experience, what many boards and executives of non-profits and governmental agencies don't appreciate is that merging or acquiring is as much about *combining intent* (purpose, value and roles) as it is about *combining assets* (balance sheet assets, cashflows and contracts, service models and methodologies, management systems, customers and goodwill). Both require careful, and separate, examination. One way I encourage my clients to think about such opportunities is to lay out two strips of paper, with the centre overlapping, or draw these on a whiteboard. We start our questioning at the (overlapping) centre, and as we work outwards, the merger questions become more challenging.

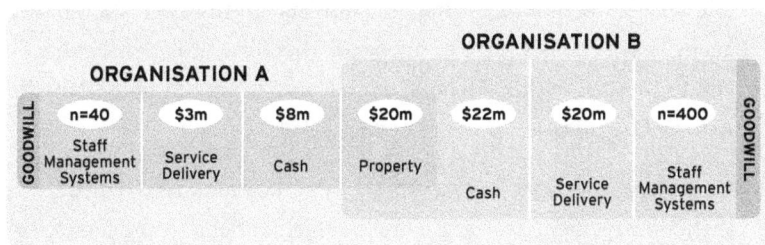

The two organisations in this diagram are both employment agencies servicing similar, but not the same, target audiences. Organisation A is quite small, with revenues of just $3 million and forty staff. However, it has $8 million in cash and owns a $15 million property, on which

6   The best reference for these seemingly clickbait claims (e.g., 'Merger success is only about 50% — equivalent to a coin toss!') is KPMG's routine reports on M&A activity, for example this report on healthcare mergers: https://assets.kpmg.com/content/dam/kpmg/pdf/2012/07/taking-the-pulse-O-201106.pdf

there is a $5 million liability. Organisation B is almost ten times larger in terms of revenue and staff, and also possesses $10 million of equity in a property. Although unquantifiable, both organisations agree that Organisation B's goodwill is much stronger than Organisation A's[7].

In this case, we used the overlapping strips as follows:

1. The overlap in the centre was the combined balance sheet asset of the two entities. The question that should be asked is: How would we leverage $X million to best advantage? In this case, the organisations planned to redevelop the $20 million property into a training academy and services hub for their target audiences.

2. Working outwards, the service delivery components give rise to these questions: What can be compatibly merged? What services are complementary? And, more importantly: Can we leverage compatible services without merging or acquiring? In this case, the smaller agency's contracts expire in one year. Therefore, it is hardly beneficial to merge for this purpose, as the contract could potentially be won by Organisation B in the open market.

3. Continuing to work outwards, the organisations next considered their management systems. These are personnel and processes, including data and technology. The same questions exist as in the previous step: What can be compatibly merged? What management or systems are complementary? And, more importantly: Can we leverage compatible management systems without merging or acquiring? In this case, Organisation B has considerably more sophisticated

---

7 Goodwill is usually characterised as the value of a company's brand name, solid customer base, good customer relations, good employee relations, and any intellectual property that can be monetised.

FROM IMPOSSIBLE TO POSSIBLE

systems, and almost none of Organisation A's systems would be carried across to a merged entity.

4. Finally, we're at the edges of our diagram, considering the goodwill factors. These include both external (customer goodwill) and internal (workplace culture) factors. The question here is: What goodwill is transferrable to a merged entity? Organisation A has weak customer goodwill, but strong workplace culture. In contrast, Organisation B has very strong customer goodwill, and moderately strong workplace culture. This suggests that a merger would benefit Organisation B's customers, but at a cost to Organisation A's staff, some or all of whom may not elect to continue with the merged entity.

At a minimum, an exercise such as this one will demonstrate whether the aims of a merger or acquisition can in fact be realised before a merger or acquisition takes place! In this case, these organisations elected not to merge, but simply wait out the end of the contract term for Organisation A. In the meantime, they entered a joint venture on just the property development. I am a conservative when it comes to merging, and would caution most of my clients to think carefully before expensive and potentially distracting due diligence is undertaken.

Frequently asked questions

There are three questions my clients often ask me about scaling:

1. **What if we're in contestable environments and can't simply scale at will?**

   Oh, you mean like aged care? Or allied health? Or affordable housing? I suggest that's structurally no different from private childcare, private medical care or private housing. They also compete in contestable environments, in which businesses are delivering largely undifferentiated products. As long as you are *not regulated out of markets* (whereby you are allocated business or must operate territorially), you can always do the following:

- Understand the business rules set by the central authority and, if possible, predict changes.

- Maximise the ability of users to choose you, especially if you are competing in a sector that offers low barriers to change providers (home-based aged care is a low barrier; residential aged care is a high barrier).

- Form strong partnerships with the various intermediaries who exist to inform consumer choice (such as referrers) or balance supply and demand in the system.

- Be aware which end of the value chain you are competing in, whether it's cost (this is at the bottom end, and includes things like cleaning) or value (this is at the top end, and includes things like behaviour support).

- Remain conscious of your competitors, whether they are non-profit, for-profit, or hybrid models (for example, non-profits acting like commercial businesses, or vice versa).

2. **Should all organisations grow? Is there ever an argument to NOT grow?**

Think about EACH (which turns over $100 million), IHI ($50 million) and even DFS ($20 million). If they were one-tenth their size (which they all were at one point), what *reach* would they have? Less than a tenth, I'd suggest. What *influence* would they have with policymakers, and other investors and funders? Much less than a tenth. What *leverage* would they be able to exert with channel partners and those who can offer adjacent services? Again, much less than a tenth.

One of my clients once said to me, 'Andrew, when we were at $5 million, we were ignored. When we were at $20 million, we were invited to meetings. Now we're at $100 million, we get to create the invite list for the meetings. We can't be ignored.' Don't argue that you shouldn't scale, simply because you're in a zone of certainty and can't work out how to build the capability to grow in significant jumps. If you've assessed the market and it's clear that your best contribution is a highly niched offering, which is genuinely different from everything else out there, make a conscious decision to focus on that niche. Otherwise, build up the seven bases, and consider merging or acquiring strategically compatible businesses to attain the next level of necessary skills. You owe it to those who don't yet benefit from your excellent work.

3. **Should we consider growing by taking over or merging with a much weaker organisation?**

    Rarely. At times, mergers do occur from positions of weakness – one entity will go out of business if it is not 'rescued' via a merger. Sometimes this is requested by a funder. At other times, clients will miss out on vital services, and the rescuing organisation makes a 'mercy dash' to provide needed services. In most cases, however, a rescue merger is to be avoided unless the 'troubled' agency has intellectual property, management systems or customers desired by the 'healthy' agency.

ACTION TO TAKE

You should always start by asking: Why grow? Don't assume you **should** grow, but certainly don't assume you shouldn't either! If you get a compelling justification for growth (usually it's maximising your reach, influence, effectiveness or quality), then:

1. Test your people's appetite for growth. Are they entrenched in a zone of certainty, or happy to move outside it? You can test this very simply by asking them: What is our ideal size? Why?

2. Determine the best scaling approach for your purpose. Check that the way you intend to grow is best suited to your role as well.

3. Using the seven bases, determine which bases are your strongest, and which are your weakest. Discuss with internal experts how you can improve.

4. Identify suitable merger and acquisition targets. Even if you decide not to take a formal approach, a simple 'thought exercise' reveals many useful insights about your strategic advantages, and how these might combine with those of others.

CHAPTER 4:

What are your goals?

ANDREW'S OBSERVATION: Many public value organisations operate on the basis of incumbency. That is, they exist because they are authorised to, not because they are working towards something specific. Even those that do have a specific purpose often don't have clear goals, or they focus solely on goals that they are funded, or contracted or legislated, to deliver. They measure what they CAN measure, not what they WANT to measure.

Many of my public sector clients seem envious of their private sector colleagues. 'They have it easy', they say to me. 'All they need to do is count profits or productivity. Everything can be measured quantitatively. We're not driven by money as a purpose, and what counts as productivity for us isn't often measurable.' Are they right?

It's true that Amazon's success is assessed at board level on factors such as market share, time from order to delivery, and out-of-stock items. These are all very tangible. But are they the most meaningful measures of success? For Amazon, the answer is: Yes, these are among them. They are essential concerns for Amazon's board, who want assurance that their purpose, pivot point and problems are being successfully addressed. But what do measures of success look like for a non-profit, especially one whose work is far less concrete than shipping stuff in boxes? In this chapter, I'll show you how to set what I refer to as minimalist goals, enabling you to focus on the things that matter most.

Setting minimalist goals

There are four reasons why I believe it is essential to arrive at a small number of minimalist goals. First, as Albert Einstein said: 'Not everything that can be counted counts.' Setting a small number of minimalist goals can help you work out what counts – politically, from a customer viewpoint, and organisationally. Second, high-level goals unify people across organisational boundaries. When well crafted, they stop people burrowing into their silos and announcing, 'We're successful!' when all they've done is implement a program, build an IT system or reduce recruitment lead times. These are all important, but they are not the vital signs of success. Third, you can refer to these minimalist goals to seek out the most potent ways to improve – simply look at those goals you're nowhere near achieving. And last, there's an old adage that is true in most organisations: What gets measured happens.

I once worked with a state-level justice department whose primary job is to run and oversee all offender programs, including prisons, community corrections and sheriffs (who ensure people fulfil debt obligations for things like traffic fines and meet other legal commitments). Typically, a department like this would have hundreds of board-level reportables. But I asked a very simple question: Which are the *most* important?

After literally days of debate, it turns out that there are four that are more important than any others:

1. Parolees complete their orders. Why? Because the community judges the department on one primary factor: Whether it has accurately gauged whether a serious offender is able to return to the community without reoffending and returning to prison.

2. Reduced recidivism (reoffending). Why? Because every four per cent added to the recidivism rate means the state has to fund another prison.

3. Reduce Aboriginal overrepresentation. Why? Because Aboriginal people are seven times more likely than the non-Aboriginal population to serve prison time.

4. Reduce family violence among case-managed men. Why? Because this is long recognised as a 'sleeper'; a highly stigmatised and under-reported crime of epidemic proportions, which has ruinous social consequences for victims, perpetrators and their children.

Each type of organisation has different ways of arriving at its three, four or ten highest-order result areas. Here is another example from a health service that honed in on just four basic goals. Radiating out from these four goals are the key success measures the organisation should focus on.

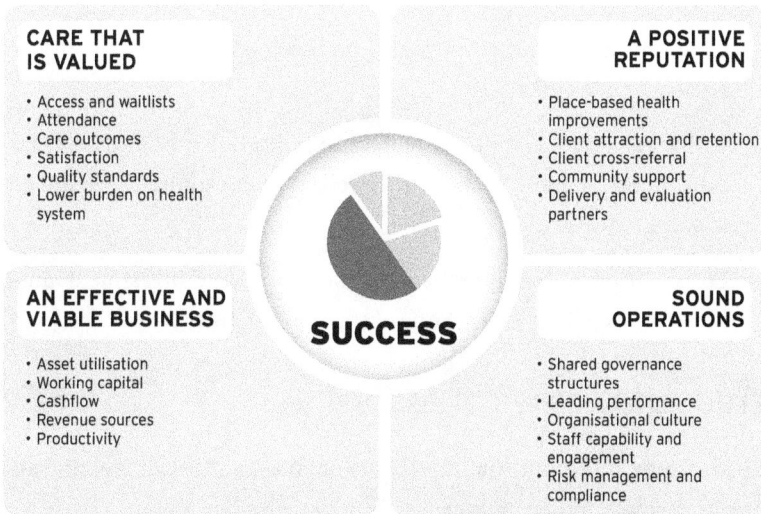

CARE THAT IS VALUED
- Access and waitlists
- Attendance
- Care outcomes
- Satisfaction
- Quality standards
- Lower burden on health system

A POSITIVE REPUTATION
- Place-based health improvements
- Client attraction and retention
- Client cross-referral
- Community support
- Delivery and evaluation partners

AN EFFECTIVE AND VIABLE BUSINESS
- Asset utilisation
- Working capital
- Cashflow
- Revenue sources
- Productivity

SUCCESS

SOUND OPERATIONS
- Shared governance structures
- Leading performance
- Organisational culture
- Staff capability and engagement
- Risk management and compliance

Focusing on the things that matter most means:

- Your staff have focus. They put effort into the most important things, and suggest innovations that directly lead to results in these areas.
- You have more influence with funders and investors, because they can be convinced of your impact, and also that your organisation is well run.

- The right capabilities can be developed, because you know what skills and systems contribute to which results.

So, Amazon would say, 'We are successful when market share grows, time from order to delivery shrinks, and out-of-stock items are as close to zero as possible.' The state justice department would say, 'We are successful when people stay out of prison once they've served their initial sentence, especially Aboriginal and family violence offenders.' If you have six to twelve key goals (rather than fifty, or 100 or 200, as I've encountered) you can:

- Count what counts (to customers, to the community, to the organisation, and politically).

- Unify your people's efforts (across organisational boundaries, because most of these higher-order result areas require departments to work together).

- Focus on areas for improvement (because every investment must move the needle in at least one of these result areas).

Frequently asked questions

There are six questions that my clients often ask me about creating appropriate goals and result areas.

1. How important is it to 'count stuff'? Should we opt for targets, or not?

Many of the world's highest-impact public value organisations count their impact. Fred Hollows counts lots of things. In 2015 alone, the organisation performed 890,066 eye operations and treatments, screened more than 3.4 million people, treated more than 8.2 million people with antibiotics for trachoma, trained 64,613 people, including

232 surgeons and 35,185 community health workers, built 110 medical facilities and supplied $2.4 million of medical equipment. Are these all valid result areas? Absolutely. Some of these are end-states (the number of people with improved eyesight), while others are factors that the foundation deems critical to achieving this.

So, should you set targets? I would argue yes, if all of the following four conditions apply to you:

- **Baseline.** That you can measure a starting position for the result you're trying to achieve.

- **Impetus.** That the setting of targets will dramatically heighten buy-in, and you can build a tracking and feedback system that enables the long-term motivation to succeed.

- **Realistic aspiration.** That you are realistic about the target you set, and how you'll reach it.

- **Leverage.** That the target, once achieved (or even on its way to being achieved), can be recognised, publicised and promoted for leverage. In other words, that it will lead to greater awareness, more uptake among target audiences, changes in policy or practice, and so on.

2. **Should we aim to quantify things that are not easily measurable?**

Yes, if you can. While this is imprecise, in some sectors this is accepted and even compelling. For instance, educational attainment (which refers to the highest level of education an individual has completed) is widely measured by attendance (or engagement, as it's becoming known) and completion by year level. Non-profits such as the Hester Hornbrook Academy, Teach For All (based in the US) and The Smith Family all have similar purposes (providing opportunities for young people who cannot easily participate in high-quality education). They all therefore judge their success on variants of school advancement and, ultimately, completion, *compared to alternatives.*

In Nepal for example, Teach For All measures the percentage of children in its schools who pass school leaving certificates (seventy-three per cent) compared to non-TFA schools (thirty-three per cent). In the US, maths students advance 2.6 months faster per year when they are in TFA-led classrooms, compared to students in non-TFA-led classrooms. So, my advice is to definitely ask this question: What evidence could we provide that our programs work *better than if we didn't exist?*

3. **Is it acceptable to measure impact by number of people helped, rather than measuring the quality of the impact itself?**

Yes. Lots of organisations, including the Fred Hollows Foundation, do this. Of course, they publish case studies (more on that in Chapter 12), but they essentially measure reach. That is, how many people did we benefit? Plenty of organisations do that in the absence of the much harder qualitative 'counting' that would be needed to fully explain impact.

Kiva is a micro-finance provider with the purpose of creating economically sustainable entrepreneurs in developing nations. It counts countries (over eighty, on five continents), borrowers (more than 2.5 million entrepreneurs have taken out no-interest loans), and total amount loaned (as at 2017, over $1 billion). These are impressive numbers, but they must act as proxies for the real impact, which is the human effects of businesses started that now support innumerable families, especially those led by women.

Similarly, the RSPCA has its well-known purpose of defending animals against cruelty, or, to put it another way, to protect the five freedoms of animals (freedom from hunger and thirst; from discomfort; from pain, injury or disease; from fear and distress; and the freedom to express normal behaviour). The RSPCA counts the number of animals helped, which, since 2009, includes about one million hens and another one million pigs.

My advice to clients is to aggregate such numbers where you can, as these numbers can impress, but remain aware that the full story needs to be told in other ways. Also, be aware that numbers can be 'gamed', or can even obscure the full story. For instance, Guide Dogs Victoria widely and successfully tells its story of guide animals (in the state, it's been the No 1 Most Trusted Charity three years in a row), but many people are surprised to discover that even with almost half-a-million low vision people, there are only 270 active guide dogs in the entire state, with about seventy trained each year[8].

4. **What if our work is not the only contributor to our purpose, or a specific outcome?**

This is very common with all forms of public value. For example, Teach For All proudly points to the fact that when it began operations in the UK, London schools were the nation's worst performing. Since 2002, TFA has placed 3,500 teachers in the capital, and has built a substantial leadership cohort, especially in disadvantaged areas, with the aim of 'detoxifying teaching for Britain's most talented graduates'. Now, in 2017, London's schools are the nation's best performing. Is TFA solely responsible? Of course not. But can it justifiably take some of the credit? Absolutely. Similarly, 350.org is an environmental grassroots move-

---

8   See Guide Dogs Victoria Annual Report, highlights of which are in a summary poster: https://www.guidedogsvictoria.com.au/wp-content/uploads/2016/07/GDV_Annual-Report_A1_Poster_594x841mm_v8_pf.pdf

ment with a lofty purpose: Solving the climate crisis. It has one stated result area, which reflects the name of the organisation: To reduce the amount of carbon dioxide in the atmosphere from its current levels of 400 parts per million to below 350 parts per million. It works with all manner of contributors (including activist groups like the Sierra Club, and media outlets like *The Guardian*) to make this happen. So, yes, think big, and enlist powerful supporters wherever you can. Just make sure you all take the credit!

5. **Is it okay to describe our impact from the customer's point of view?**

Yes, always. In many ways, this is the most potent way of both thinking about, and reporting, results. Beyondblue is an Australian awareness-raising organisation with the purpose of improving mental health for all. It notes that, in Australia alone, two million people suffer anxiety, one million struggle with depression, and fifty commit suicide every week. Clearly, the organisation can't reach these people in such numbers. But what it can do is count its reach. In 2016, 160,000 people used beyondblue's support methods (a telephone helpline as well as online forums).

Of greater interest is the way the organisation measures impact for those people. Sixty-seven per cent of the respondents felt less depressed or anxious, thirty-eight per cent connected with a health professional as a direct result of using the website's forums, and sixty-nine per cent stated they had initiated a positive lifestyle change, such as opting for a healthier diet and exercising. With these results, beyondblue has earned the confidence of all levels of government, and is widely recognised by Australians.

You can, and should, establish whether the benefit you provide for your customers is quantifiable by considering four factors, in order of impact. Imagine, for example, your organisation's purpose is to help people with financial stresses reclaim economic power, and your role is to provide financial education. Here are the four factors you'd need to consider:

- **Reach.** The number of people who open your newsletters or watch your YouTube videos.

- **Uptake.** The number of people who respond in some practical way, like attending an event, completing an e-learning program, filling in a diagnostic, or participating in a support program.

- **Behavioural change.** The number and types of changes to behaviour that eventuate from your interventions. For instance, increased ability to calculate expenses and income or build a basic investment plan.

- **Results.** The proof that someone has reclaimed economic power. For example, money saved, or debts paid off.

6. **What if all our result areas are positive, except the ones we can't influence?**

IPC Health delivers some forty different services to a large metropolitan area and, of forty result areas in four broad categories, it has achieved its quantifiable goals in thirty-seven. The remaining three, however, are proving very difficult to budge. They are waitlists, unmet demand and avoidable hospital admissions. Are these failures on the part of IPC Health? Only partly. Largely, they do not fall within the organisation's control or capabilities under the existing health system settings.

This signals that a potential result area for IPC Health's future may be its level of influence. In other words, it may choose to measure changes (that it recommends) to adjacent services that absorb demand away from IPC Health. Or it may measure policy or funding formula changes (again, that it recommends), which deliver greater service capacity.

ACTION TO TAKE

To become a best-of-breed public value organisation, engage your team in the following conversations:

1. Can we identify the four to eight most critical result areas? Why are these the most critical?

2. Can we describe our desired end-state from the customer's perspective? ('We are successful when our customers are/do/have/can X.')

3. Can we track how many people we benefit? (This number won't tell the whole story, but it will support your claims of high impact.)

4. What are the flow-on impacts of our goals? ('When our customer can be/do/have X, it results in Y.')

5. And, finally, be clear about what's measurable today, what's going to be measurable within a year (if you set up baselining and measurement systems now), and what is likely to elude you for some time, unless you invest significantly in measurement, assessment or research, either by yourselves, or in partnership. ('We would love to be able to measure our impact in X, but won't be able to until Y.')

CHAPTER 5:

What are your values?

ANDREW'S OBSERVATION: I see a paradox. Every public value organisation is values-based and uses its core principles to differentiate
itself from others, especially for-profit organisations. Yet, relatively
few can articulate these principles. They are either bland, boring, bu-
reaucratised or banal. Or, organisations are doing powerful work, with
plenty of passion, yet can't codify how and why this works.

Just like the most successful brands, the highest-impact public value
organisations attribute their success to a strong culture. But what is a
strong culture? I've long observed that strong cultures exist where people are very clear about the beliefs that, when shared, predict success.
Southwest Airlines has had two clearly defined values since its inception: Low-cost flights and happy customers. Herb Kelleher was always
open to new ideas, partly because he had a simple test for them: 'How
will this help us be the lowest-cost airline? How will it help people be
tremendously satisfied with us?' The art here is that he recognised that
these values pull against each other. He could have easily found cost-
cutting measures that destroyed customer confidence, and he could
have pleased customers in ways that sent him broke.

As we've already seen, Fred Hollows has prevented avoidable blindness
in millions of people in Vietnam, Nepal and outback Australia with two
mantras that were hardwired from himself into his team. First, that a
basic attribute of humankind is to look after each other. Second, that re-
storing sight is akin to total transparency and full visibility. This means
his organisation has always had a clear, compelling message for donors,
partners and governments, which has greatly assisted its impact.

So, even if your purpose and role are fungible (meaning that, on the surface, you're pretty much the same as everyone else and therefore interchangeable), it might well be that your culture is unique, or at least distinctive. In that case, your values will be your differentiator. That means moving beyond values as bland statements on laminated posters in hallways, which people hurriedly pass by. It means a lot more than reading some slides to your staff during induction, and then hoping they remember some sort of acronym that spells out something clever or memorable. It means more than asking your HR people to provide 'values elicitation workshops' as part of your annual cycle of compliance training.

In this chapter, I'll show you how to come up with a set of values that truly guide what your organisation will and won't do. We'll turn our attention to a household tech name that did this exceptionally well, and then to a grassroots community organisation that is gaining national recognition in Australia for its values-based culture.

Using values as a differentiator

Reed Hastings, founder of Netflix, famously developed a constantly changing slide-deck for his organisation simply titled 'Netflix Culture: Freedom and Responsibility'. Here are some of the key insights:

1. When you've identified the five to ten values that drive the success of your organisation (however you define it), you must then hire and promote those people who demonstrate these values.

2. Values are key to the 'keeper test'. In other words, you want every employee to be someone you'd fight to keep.

3. Values are nothing other than helping each other be great.

Netflix doesn't have values as a bland philosophy, but instead puts considerable effort into using them as a differentiator. It does this by insisting on its core philosophy of people over process. Just read these value statements and consider whether they mark out a very different organisation from the majority of large corporations:

- We encourage independent decision making by employees.
- We share information openly, broadly and deliberately.
- We are extraordinarily candid with each other.
- We keep only our highly effective people.
- We avoid rules.

Later in this chapter, I'll talk about how to use such statements as powerful tools for shaping the behaviours within your organisation.

Another organisation that uses values as a differentiator, and has done this remarkably successfully, is Sunbury Community Health in Victoria. When asked about his proudest achievement, CEO Phillip Ripper could point to the fact that his organisation has won the prestigious Health Service of the Year award – twice in a row. He could also point to the fact that Sunbury is in the black on all services, and that its equity position has improved fifty per cent in three years. Instead, his greatest pride comes from the fact that his staff developed and internalised a set of values that is the guiding light for how they approach their work.

Sunbury Community Health's purpose is: 'A community whose social fabric and wellbeing is strong.' When I started working with Phil and his team, they were keen to move from a cottage industry of passionate community developers to a more professional and business-like footing. There were two conditions on my brief. First, they didn't know what a 'business-like' footing actually looked like for their sort of organisation.

Second, they would not tolerate any dilution of their values to achieve better operating results. Phil also wanted to find a way to capture the 'secret sauce' that was Sunbury's most potent force for good.

At first, we spoke with staff in groups and went through various iterations of the question: What beliefs do you share that genuinely create social fabric? We ended up with something like this:

- Future focus
- Authenticity and integrity
- Collaboration
- Achievement

Does any of that look familiar? Yes, it's the same as pretty much any (bland) values set from a public value organisation (and plenty of for-profits as well). It didn't stick, wasn't memorable, and staff felt it was impersonal. So, we decided to hand the process over to the entire staff of 150, with minimal guidance. All we said was: 'It's got to be plain English, we must be able to remember them all, our clients' eyes have got to light up when we explain them, and it's got to show how we're different from everyone else.'

The staff went away and reverse-engineered what they felt made them special. This is what they came up with:

- It takes a village to belong and grow.
- Passionately engaged with our community, and with each other.
- We do the right thing, not just the easy thing.
- We make things happen; we get things done.

This harnessed so much energy that staff started to hold meetings, unbidden by their managers, to discuss these one at a time. They printed the values not on wall posters (which is what everyone else does), but on decorative pot plants. At their own expense, they printed four types of T-shirts (one for each value) and coordinated wearing these on separate days. Yes, it sounds cheesy, but the way in which staff galvanised their effort around these values was truly remarkable. And that's why it brings a tear to Phil's eye when he talks about what makes him proud as a chief executive. Because values are never about the leader; they're about 'helping each other be great', as Reed Hastings would say.

That sounds like the end of the story, but it isn't. As the organisation was questioning its difference, it became obvious that it had to answer a very public question: What *aren't* we? And so it discussed how its twenty-four service areas, which are a mix of clinical, medical and social services, are completely unlike those of for-profit health clinics.

Here's a partial list of what it came up with:

WE DON'T JUST FOCUS ON...	WE CARE ABOUT...
our clients individually	our entire community's health, and connecting the unconnected
disease and ill health	the factors that predict whether a person or community is healthy
patient throughput	the whole context of a person's health
addressing specific problems	supporting or strengthening people and communities
being 'the experts'	using our expertise to help others
reacting to problems after they've happened	preventing problems, by teaching and showing
transactions with customers or patients	real relationships, with multiple touchpoints
service delivery	guiding and modelling
episodic care, with single interventions	addressing people's complex and multifaceted needs

Phil is justifiably proud of the fact that Sunbury has gone from having no formal strategy, no way of measuring its results, and no prioritisation of effort to being one of his state's recognised leaders, without any loss of what makes the organisation special. Phil says, 'We went from a feel-good community organisation where, out of 100 staff, only two knew how to use a spreadsheet, to a community business where everyone understands our seventeen objectives, how we measure them, and how our values work against each and every one of these.'

Frequently asked questions

Here are five common questions about values that I get from my clients.

1. **What's the difference between values, or principles, and philosophies?**

   None. I use these terms interchangeably because they all refer to fundamentals that are held jointly among people united for a common cause. With my clients, I define values as 'shared beliefs that predict success'. I don't mind what my clients call them at all.

2. **How long should it take to develop values? How many should we have?**

   It won't take long if you do what one New Zealand non-profit did in 2010. It ended up with eleven values (yes, eleven!), each with five dot points. Zeal general manager Elliot Taylor talked about the organisation's first hui (a Maori word for 'assembly') and how the team simply brainstormed on a whiteboard. 'There were about fifty bullet points. Words like innovative, initiative, honesty, compassionate, questioner, humility and risk-taker. There were also sketches of an elephant head, a bicep flexing, a smiling flower and what looks like an early iteration of the poop emoji. Whoever that was, I salute your pioneering vision.'[9] Now, almost a decade later, Zeal has found just four 'banner values' that Elliot believes are incredibly enduring: Passionate, creative, innovative and inclusive. These work for Zeal, because with growth come inevitable questions, starting with: Should we…? Instead, to add urgency and potency to the question (so it's not merely an option!), I advise my clients to reference their own values, and turn the question into: Must we…?

3. Once we have agreed values, how should we actually use them?

Have you ever seen a hologram? It's a three-dimensional image formed from light sources by a laser. What many people don't know about holograms is that if you snip one in half, you don't get half an image – you get a whole image, just smaller. All the information from the whole image is coded into that piece. You can continue doing that over and over, until you have just a tiny fragment, but still containing the entire image – just smaller and at lower resolution.

Values are like holograms. However small an interaction someone has with your organisation, your full set of values should be visible. Your values are visible whenever I phone with an enquiry, meet with your staff, look at your website, enter your buildings, work as a project partner, or participate in a project you lead. All of them. All of the time. In a more practical sense, values should be the reference point for key decisions, especially:

- Who to hire, and who to fire.

- How to develop people.

- Who to promote and who to reward.

9   http://zeal.nz/blog/how-we-discovered-zeals-people-values-and-what-they-actually-are

- Who to partner with, acquire or merge with (we'll discuss this in more detail in Chapter 11).

- What investment or funding to accept, with what conditions.

4. What should I do if I observe breaches of our values?

There are two types of breaches: Strategic breaches (you've failed to set up the necessary context and conditions) and behavioural breaches (the conditions exist, but people still don't represent the values). A government department I once worked with had 'innovation' as a published value. When I talked to their customers and stakeholders, I heard that this department's officers were rigid, process-bound and inflexible. If a matter was outside policy, it wouldn't be entertained. I went back and asked the C-suite leaders this question: 'I understand you value innovation. Am I right?' There was a straightening of ties and a few glances around the table, before one of the executives spoke up. 'Yes, Andrew, that's correct. We believe in being responsive to changing needs, and therefore continually seek to improve our processes.' Ugh. This response indicated there was certainly a breach.

Next came a question to determine whether it was a strategic breach or a behavioural breach: 'Can you tell me a little about how much time you give to innovation and who leads it, and provide three recent examples?' They would have no trouble answering this question if they had three things in place: *Time* set aside for innovation processes, projects that were explicitly *labelled* 'innovations', and *authorisation* that enabled tolerance of the downside of a value (in this case, tolerance of failure). But they had none of this, resulting in a strategic breach. Because they hadn't set a context for innovation, they shifted uncomfortably in their seats and made various justifications.

To avoid a strategic breach, each of your values requires context in the following areas: Time and process, labels and naming, and authorisations and permissions. These apply whatever your final banner values are.

If, however, you have a context for innovation that's well supported, but one part of the organisation is not perceived to be innovative, then you have a *behavioural* breach. Then, you need to ensure you are providing the right practical reinforcement for the value expected. (In Chapter 9, you'll learn how to set the right strategic context and behavioural reinforcement for innovation in public value organisations.)

5. Can values ever be contentious?

Of course. All revolutions are conflicts of values! Whether that's a corporate board takeover or a political uprising. In fact, you know your values are striking a chord if people object to them, or even threaten to resign. Patrick Lencioni, who wrote *The Five Dysfunctions of a Team*, says, 'If you're not willing to accept the pain real values incur, don't bother going to the trouble of formulating a values statement.'[10] The key is to have far more people who are supportive of those values and passionate about upholding them. Lencioni differentiates three types of values: Core values are emblematic of an organisation's culture (like 'the HP Way' at Hewlett-Packard); permission-to-play values are what you expect from every employee all the time (like integrity, or respect); and aspirational values are those which do not represent the current culture, but you want and need them to. Aspirational values typically include innovation, urgency, speed, efficiency, customer-focus and creativity. When investigated, and the context is set for these (time and process, labels and naming, and authorisations

10 Lencioni, Patrick (2002) 'Make Your Values Mean Something', *Harvard Business Review*

and permissions), then conflicts can and must arise. Don't despair when this happens – this is a sign of health!

ACTION TO TAKE

If values are shared beliefs that predict your success, you need to articulate what those shared beliefs are. If you don't, or your people don't, you must invest time, money and effort in this. You can start to refine (or build from scratch) your values with questions like these:

1. What are three specific instances of our greatest success, and what beliefs have created this success?

2. What are we doing that doesn't serve us well? What beliefs are no longer useful to us? What beliefs will be helpful to us in future?

3. What are we not? How are we different from others?

Then, once you've got answers to these questions, you can test them by asking:

4. Do these resonate? Are they expressed in plain English, not bland corporate-speak? (Have another look at the value statements of Sunbury and Netflix.)

Once you have a workable (but not necessarily final) list to work with, then ask yourselves:

5. What do we need to do to set a context for these values in the areas of time and process, labels and naming, and authorisation and permissions?

6. How will we ensure these values are being displayed? How will we 'call it out' when they're not?

CHAPTER 6:

Gaining traction

ANDREW'S OBSERVATION: Public value organisations sometimes invest big dollars and lots of time into developing the 'right' strategy; by answering questions of purpose, role, values, goals and scale. But then the strategy sits on the shelf, and the activity of the organisation bears little relationship to the strategy. I frequently notice that strategy formation is the easy part; strategy internalisation is far harder, and where organisations typically need more help.

Not long ago, I was in conversation with a CEO who was complaining that some of her thirty-strong management team 'just aren't getting it'. When I asked what they weren't 'getting', she said, 'The whole strategy. The why. The what. The how. They're just running their operations the same as they always did. I'm not seeing any change!'

'Do you mean literally all managers?' I asked.

She replied, 'No, just some of them, if I'm honest.'

'And on all aspects of your new strategy?'

'Well, probably not. But who knows, really?'

Who knows, indeed.

Finally, I asked her, 'What if you had a simple way to gauge which of your managers are sold, which are on the fence and what it would take to get them over the fence, and which aren't sold at all and why? Would that be worth a simple twenty-minute conversation with each of them?'

In this final chapter of Part 1, I'll show you how to form strategy with your team, and then test their understanding, acceptance and commitment to that strategy.

Discovering where and how to apply your energies

Successful strategy internalisation is determined by energy. While Amazon's strategy is a set of insights about how it will become (and remain) the dominant online retailer, the successful internalisation of its strategy is whether it provides a framework for decision making. In other words, it's whether Amazon's strategy enables a series of choices about where and how to apply its energies (a catch-all term I'll use for all forms of capital or resourcing, whether it's people, money, knowledge, buildings, or community mobilisation and support). We saw earlier that Amazon's strategy is to fulfil online orders in a way that solves three problems for its customers:

1. More choice

2. Greater convenience

3. Lower prices

But Amazon recognises that it has a critical weakness to overcome – that people have to wait for their orders. It has therefore built its strategy *around a single pivot point*: Fulfil orders as fast as possible, so as to reduce the lag time in online shopping. This pivot point, if achieved, will determine Amazon's success. If it isn't achieved, Amazon will fail. Simple. Amazon then internalises the pivot point by setting objectives around the percentage of orders that will be delivered the same day they're made (in some cases, within an hour), while a sizeable minority will be shipped within two days. Furthermore, Amazon's internalisation strategy asks another question: In what do we need to invest time, money and effort, so that we can dramatically shorten delivery times?

The answer to that question is three things:

1. Putting fulfilment centres (Amazon's term for warehouses) at the crossroads of logistics corridors (air and road) and in close relation to where the customers are located.

2. Automating everything. By that, I mean ensuring that robots do anything physical, and that computers do anything cognitive. Humans are only useful for physical and cognitive tasks that robots and computers can't do.

3. Building out a dense mesh of pick-up partners. These deal with the dilemma of the customer not being at the drop-off location (such as their home). Instead, Amazon will deliver to any place that is open or accessible twenty-four hours a day, seven days a week (like a locker at a petrol station), in the natural pathway of the customer (in other words, somewhere they'd go anyway, like a supermarket) or, even better, somewhere they already are (for example, Amazon is experimenting with making deliveries to car boots by gaining customers' permission to access their GPS location and electronic boot release).

In contrast, what I see some public value organisations doing is the opposite of a clear and sharp view about where to invest their energies. Not long ago, I was discussing a potential strategy project with a client. One of the senior staff, whose title was Director of Strategy, came to an initial meeting with the organisation's strategic plans. Yes, plural. The plans were in binders. Yes, plural. I'd estimate a metre of shelf space, in fact. I tactfully had to explain that strategy is not a plan (or many plans). Strategy is a set of insights from which you create a framework for decision making. A plan is a detailed proposal for doing something and a means to assign responsibilities for this.

Of course, it's not the Director of Strategy's job to singlehandedly devise and implement a strategy. Rather, the Director of Strategy – along with the organisation's chief executive and board (if there is one) – should engage as many useful informants in the process as possible to provide the most valuable insights. There's an art to working out who to involve, when, and for what purpose.

Here's what that process looked like to replace the binders with a well-informed and well-internalised strategy. We constructed a matrix which shows the form of consultation (across the top), and the widest range of informants who could provide useful insights to inform the organisation's strategy (down the left-hand side).

	PURPOSE	VALUES	ROLE	IDEAL CUSTOMER	GOALS	SCALE	PRIORITIES	ENABLERS
Non-executive directors				1				
Executives								6
Staff and content experts					2			
Customers			3					
Community	4							
Stakeholders, investors, partners					5			

The shaded cells of the matrix show which informants should contribute to which questions. The numbers then indicate the sequence of activities across the timeline from left to right. Dark grey indicates *contributors* (those who have an interest in the outcome, such as users, owners or others who have accountability for results) while the pale grey indicates *validators* (those who have a unique perspective and therefore may add important distinctions to the ideas being formed). The numbers refer to my preferred sequence of getting the information. I always start with bringing directors (board members) and executives together for big-picture scoping, before moving to staff, customers, community and other stakeholders.

Three ways to simplify your strategy

Notice that, so far, we've focused on internalisation while strategy is being formed. What about after it is authorised by the board, and formally adopted? What then? My strong belief is that after formal adoption, internalisation is effective when three things happen to dramatically simplify the strategy.

TALK ABOUT WHAT'S NOT GOING TO CHANGE

This should happen constantly and consistently. Many leaders are very adept at describing changes, but Amazon's Jeff Bezos takes a different approach: 'I very frequently get the question: "What's going to change in the next ten years?" ... I almost never get the question: "What's not going to change in the next ten years?" And I submit to you that that second question is actually the more important of the two – because you can build a business strategy around the things that are stable in time.' The fundamentals that Bezos concentrates on are those that we've already discussed: Choice, price and convenience. He goes on to say, 'It's impossible to imagine a future ten years from now where a customer comes up and says, "Jeff I love Amazon; I just wish the prices were a little higher ... I just wish you'd deliver a little more slowly." ... When you have something that you know is true, even over the long term, you can afford to put a lot of energy into it.'

GET YOUR PEOPLE TO SELL TO YOUR PEOPLE

Don't rely on the usual 'talking heads' of chairman, CEO or executives. Get clinicians to convince clinicians, analysts to persuade analysts.

Everyone listens to people like themselves, and the more points of reference there are for specific messages, the harder it is to ignore those messages.

Even use customers to sell ideas. One of my clients solves problems relating to gambling, and they internalised a research strategy by having former problem gamblers talk about their downward spiral in very real ways, linking this to comments like: 'I wish we understood why people like me don't get help earlier' or 'If we knew more about why some people are drawn to addictive behaviour, and others aren't, then we'd have a better chance at stopping people like me almost killing themselves out of desperation.' This makes strategy very visceral, and draws a straight line between your strategy and its desired outcomes.

DESCRIBE IT SIMPLY

You recall the executive with the multiple binders? I looked through them, and I couldn't orient myself at all. There was no overview, no single piece of paper on which I saw the whole. All I saw were details, densely packed.

Instead, find ways to reduce your strategy and your message to simple images, categories and infographics, or engage experts to do it. There are many such models, including my own, which I call Strategy on a Page, an example of which is shown opposite. This is not intended to be read word for word. Rather, I want to show that you can display a lot of complexity in just a single page (if you want to see a fully readable version of this Strategy on a Page, go to http://workwell.com.au and look for the free resources).

Such a depiction should, at a minimum, include purpose, role, scale, goals and values. Some of my clients will also want other aspects of their directions featured, such as geographic reach, operating model, revenue models or commercial principles. The guiding principle in such depictions is: What do we want all of our people to understand about our future business?

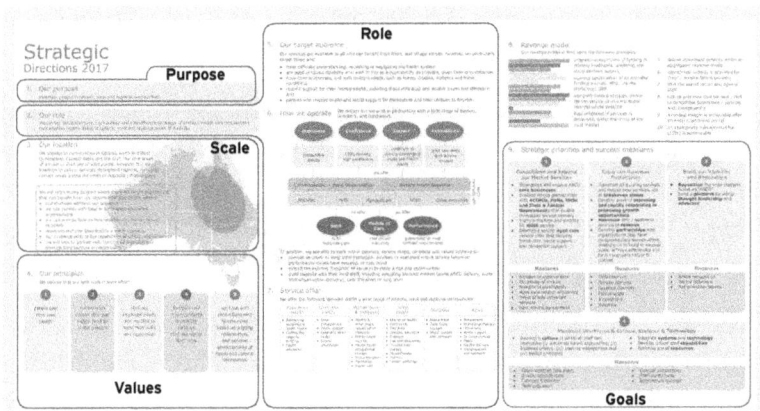

Once you've created a Strategy on a Page, there are two things you can do with it:

1. Repurpose it, for both internal and external use (such as CEO presentations, speeches and blogs; staff newsletters; round tables and staff meetings).

2. Instruct staff to 'sell' the new messages to others, namely their team members, colleagues and clients. This can be done through meetings or workshops, digitally through various social, group collaboration and project management platforms, or via internal strategic communications, such as newsletters, videos and blogs.

Assessing uptake of the new strategy

What if you're still not convinced that your strategy has traction? Do you recall Rhonda, the CEO who didn't know if her new strategy was internalised by her thirty managers? Let's pick up the conversation from earlier.

Rhonda said, 'Of course I'd be interested to know who's with me, and who's not.'

'You mean who's not with you *yet*,' I clarified.

Then, right in front of her, I sketched out a flow diagram with four vital elements (see opposite).

'The first thing you need to do is assess each manager's understanding of the change. What the rationale is, what the change consists of or the initiatives, and then the ultimate benefit to the client. You don't lecture them – you simply ask them what their understanding is, and then check the boxes. They'll tick none, some or all of them.

'Then, you can ask them about their acceptance of these changes – what they see as valuable, and what they see as the risks. You can rate these up or down depending on what they say. Finally, this is all multiplied out by the level of commitment they bring – what they're willing to promote, or what's difficult for them to support.

'Their likely action is a sum of understanding, acceptance and commitment. Those near the top are your champions. They'll be champions on your behalf. There are then realists, not as outspokenly positive, but seen as highly credible by others. Down the scale further are those you'll have to work to convert – they'll need some further convincing before they'll sign on. Finally, there are the laggards. These are the people whom you need to neutralise quickly, or they'll stall the process in their areas. If there are quite a few laggards, you might even consider pausing the whole process, as you simply will not succeed if half of your managerial layer is sitting in this category.'

Rhonda replied, 'I see what you mean. I do need to have these conversations, as I'm honestly not sure who I'd see as champions, or even how many laggards we might have. Can I take the paper with me?'

I laughed, before replying, 'I'll do you one better, Rhonda. I'll put it together as a diagnostic, and you and your executives can then have the same conversations with each of your thirty managers.'

Change Readiness Diagnostic
PROJECT: Operations Redesign

| Manager's Name: | Date: |

1 UNDERSTANDING **+ 2** ACCEPTANCE **x 3** COMMITMENT **= 4** ACTION

'What is your understanding of the changes being proposed?'

RATIONALE
- ☐ Savings: cost-base
- ☐ Savings: EBA
- ☐ Trial new initiatives that increase flexibility and efficiencies
- ☐ Eventually, reduce reliance on sites

INITIATIVES
- ☐ Replace Grade 1s with Grade 2s
- ☐ Care Team Structure
- ☐ ABCD Service cessation
- ☐ Regional 3 staff for PVP work
- ☐ Workforce Planner
- ☐ Reduce hours of P/T staff
- ☐ Standardised packages of care
- ☐ Visit routing
- ☐ Intake functions

ASSESS

BENEFIT
- ☐ Greater clarity re: time of visit
- ☐ Greater responsiveness
- ☐ Client experience is understood

INFORM

A. Explain above rationale / features / benefit that respondent does not cover, or covers inaccurately or incompletely

B. What questions do you have?

VALUE

+1 What in your opionion is the **value** of the changes?

+1 What can we do to **maximise** these?

NOTES

RISKS

-1 What, in your opinion, are the **risks** / downsides of the changes

+1 What can we do to **mitigate** these?

NOTES

+1 What can you do to **promote** the value of these changes within your team / through the org?

What aspects of the change are -1 **difficult for you to support?**

MORE ↑

12
11
10
'CHAMPION'
It's obvious that you're very enthusiastic about the changes. What can we do to help you **convey** these messages as positively as possible?

9
8
7
'REALIST'
I get the impression that you're broadly positive, but see some risks. What can we do to demonstrate that we're thinking of the redesign as **realistically** as possible?

6
5
4
'CONVERT'
I gather that you're cautiously positive. What can we do to assure you that the changes are rolled out as **sensitively** as possible?

3
2
1
0
'LAGGARD'
I get a very strong sense that you're struggling to support these changes? What, if anything, can we do to **turn you around** on this?

When you or your colleagues aren't sure whether strategy, or any change initiative, has been internalised or not, you can build your own version of this sheet. Simply plug in the dot points in the 'Assess' area on the left-hand side, and then have the necessary conversations. Don't hide your intent – tell people that you simply want to assess the realistic uptake of the new strategy. You need people to be open and honest with you in order to work out how best to proceed.

Frequently asked questions

Here are five common questions about strategy internalisation that I get from my clients:

1. What if the 'why' is out of my hands?

In government, this happens a lot. You are legislated to exist. Your purpose is handed to you on a plate. Often, politically driven 'machinery of government'[11] dictates decisions to change or merge functions. Often, the rationale for the change is not based on strong organisational or functional principles, nor is there strategic and cultural fit between functions that now have to work together. Other times, there are vast chasms that a single organisation must encompass in its purpose.

In my home state of Victoria, Australia, our state government has, over the years, gradually coalesced into a small number of mega-departments. As a result, as of 2017, we have long-winded department titles such as the Department of Economic Development, Jobs, Transport and Resources, which has a broad-ranging purpose to 'get

---

11 A phrase originating with John Stuart Mill, and used as an official term in Australia and other Commonwealth countries to refer to the changes to the structure of government, and the allocation of government functions between departments and ministers.

our economy and society working together for the benefit of all Victorians – by creating more jobs for more people, connecting people and businesses, and maintaining Victoria's envied reputation for liveability now, and for the future.'

In a case like this, the executives and leaders of this department have no choice of whether to internalise this purpose – they simply must. What they do have a choice over is how this internalisation occurs. In other words, 'more jobs for more people' has been translated as 'more people having meaningful work that is safe and secure'. In turn, this is translated further by defining the role and scope of the department: 'We do this by supporting businesses and workers, developing and growing our future industries, attracting investment to our regions and supporting industries in transition. We also create jobs by leveraging our natural assets, including fostering our visitor economy, creativity and innovation.'

The other type of public value organisation for which the 'why' is often not negotiable is venerable non-profits. The Order of Saint John of God is named after a Portuguese soldier turned healthcare worker. Since its inception in the late sixteenth century, its purpose has been hospitality, hope and healing. The brothers and nuns of the order are now substantially depleted, but the 'why' of the work continues, through its hospitals, as the largest Catholic healthcare provider in Australia, and one of the largest non-public health services in the country. Here, like in government, the 'why' is not up for questioning. However, the organisation has translated a strongly traditional Christian vision and set of values into a twenty-first century 'service ethos', which takes substantial time, money and effort to communicate to each of its 10,000+ staff.

2. How do I stop strategy being overtaken by operations?

Most organisations employ experts to do their leadership heavy lifting. Hospitals employ former clinicians, universities employ former academics, and regulators employ former engineers, finance experts or lawyers. Educational institutions employ former teachers, while human service organisations hire middle-aged social workers. These are all fine professions. However, when turning their hand to leadership, especially strategic leadership, a common fault I observe is a tendency to look first at means ('the how') and then, if at all, at the ends ('the why').

A healthcare client of mine has no fewer than six clinicians on its board (some retired, some not). When we were discussing future direction, they kept coming back to solutions (care pathways, digital health, workforce redesign) rather than asking fundamental 'why' questions (like 'What sort of perinatal care do women ideally want?' and 'What are the big end-of-life care challenges that need to be solved?').

Many professions are trained to solve problems first and foremost (not just doctors, but engineers, lawyers and architects). Therefore, the solutions will often come to them before the problem is fully defined. I encourage my clients to consciously reverse this bias by constantly referencing purpose, and, most importantly, the customer's problems. Keep asking the following questions, until you're blue in the face:

- What is the problem we are solving?
- How can we best do it?
- How will the customer know it's been solved?

Even once strategy has been formed, in my experience, most senior people (boards and executives) spend way too much time on operational matters. I often show the following diagram to my clients as a way of suggesting that at least half of their time should be spent on strategy. That includes assessing the environment, exercising foresight and forming scenarios, and then agreeing on strategy and the necessary organisational policies that provide a framework or criteria for the board's (and CEO's) decision making.

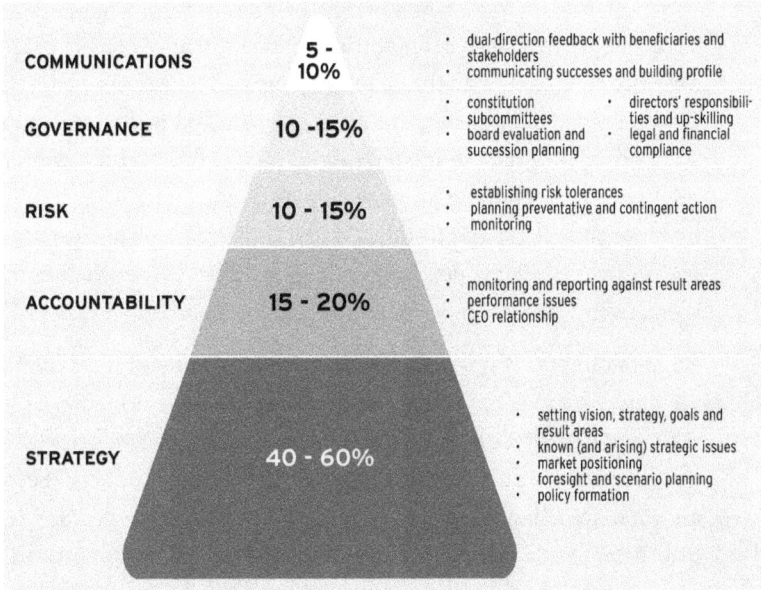

COMMUNICATIONS	**5 - 10%**	• dual-direction feedback with beneficiaries and stakeholders • communicating successes and building profile
GOVERNANCE	**10 -15%**	• constitution • directors' responsibilities and up-skilling • subcommittees • board evaluation and • legal and financial succession planning compliance
RISK	**10 - 15%**	• establishing risk tolerances • planning preventative and contingent action • monitoring
ACCOUNTABILITY	**15 - 20%**	• monitoring and reporting against result areas • performance issues • CEO relationship
STRATEGY	**40 - 60%**	• setting vision, strategy, goals and result areas • known (and arising) strategic issues • market positioning • foresight and scenario planning • policy formation

Many of my clients confess that they have reversed the ratios for accountability and strategy. They spend at least half their time getting retrospective reports on performance, and only a fifth of their time (often at a single, two-day annual retreat!) examining the strategic aspects.

You also need to keep people accountable for the results of the strategy. We'll look at that in more detail in Part 2.

3. What's the leader's job in strategy internalisation?

Every organisation is made up of leaders at the appropriate level. To the public, the chairperson is the leader. To the investors and funders, it's the chief executive. To the staff, it's general management. To the frontline staff, it's the frontline leaders, coordinators and team leaders. This means that all of these leaders have three jobs:

- **Be aligned.** The chairperson needs confidence that his or her messages are congruent with the CEO's, and onward to team leader level. The best test of alignment is to consider real (or, failing that, realistic) scenarios appropriate to the level in question. So, a board scenario might be, 'How does our strategy help us decide under what conditions we should expand to other states?', whereas a team-level scenario might be, 'How does our strategy help us decide whether to spend twenty per cent more time assisting our most complex clients?'

- **Be an example.** While few leaders of public value organisations are autocrats making unilateral decisions, there is nonetheless a real need to provide a strong reference point for decisions that the group owns. Useful framing language for such instances is: 'Let's all remember that our purpose is X and that we have decided to prioritise Y, so I'll leave it to you to consider the best approach' and 'I recently faced a dilemma where I had to ask myself whether, in keeping with our strategy, we should invest in X or Y. I decided on Y, the reason being Z.' In these cases, you are showing your willingness to take strategy by the horns and deeply interrogate its relevance, very transparently, in front of the people you lead.

- **Live in the future.** The more senior you are, the further ahead you have to live. If you're a director or CEO, it's five to ten years. If you're a general manager or executive director, it's three to five. If you're middle management, it's one to three. One of the most powerful internalisation exercises for leaders is to write the press release of the future. Imagine that, five years from now, you're talking about how your organisation has grown and improved in that time. Get your people to write these, discuss and critique them, and, finally, prepare joint versions based on everyone's best work.

4. **What if our new strategy requires new approaches, or even displaces people?**

Don't sugarcoat it. If you've engaged early, and well, smart people will see it coming. If you've done the questioning around 'Why do we exist?' and 'What problems are we solving?', people won't easily be able to argue for backwards-looking practices. If you think this is a risk because of changing policy or market conditions, try to highlight the opportunities that may arise. The most obvious case of this in Australia is the national rollout of an insurance model and a competitive market for disability supports to replace centralised government-funded models. New skills are needed, staff will be displaced, and entire units or even organisations will cease to exist or be transformed.

In such cases, I encourage my clients to develop 'testable assumptions' about the future. Such assumptions might be trends (such as 'Patients will be more active than passive in their care' or 'Team-based care will replace care by individual practitioners') or quantitative predictions ('The population will increase by twenty per cent in the next ten years, but the number of GPs will only grow by five per cent'). My guidance to my clients is to form between half-a-dozen and a dozen of these, act as if they are true, recognise opportunities in each (don't just see them as threats), and find data sources that provide evidence of whether your assumptions are correct. Then, annually, check them. Challenge each one and add new ones.

This language is important, as you are not stating unequivocally that jobs will be lost, or that roles will change. Rather, you are asking people to make an educated guess about how the future might look different. In every case, I am pleasantly surprised at how able people are to make, and accept, predictions that result in significant change. In the example I gave earlier, doctors were cautious about changes that would reduce their already stressed billing capacity. However, when they had a chance to really examine what excellent team-based care looks like, they recognised that there are, in fact, potential billing items that they could claim, resulting in higher revenues, not lower ones.

5. What's the hardest part of strategy to internalise?

Direction. It's easy to create a strategy that looks like nothing will change. Have you ever seen (or worked on) a strategy where purpose and values are motherhood statements, where the organisation's role looks exactly the same as it always has, and the priorities are simply rolled-up versions of the objectives of each business unit? In this case, the best thing you can do is create a super-simple spider diagram, like this one.

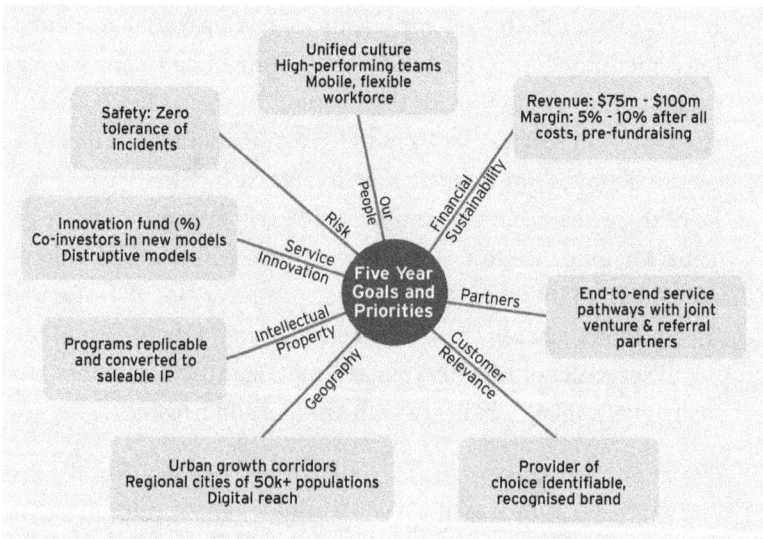

Unified culture
High-performing teams
Mobile, flexible
workforce

Safety: Zero
tolerance of
incidents

Revenue: $75m - $100m
Margin: 5% - 10% after all
costs, pre-fundraising

Innovation fund (%)
Co-investors in new models
Distruptive models

End-to-end service
pathways with joint
venture & referral
partners

Programs replicable
and converted to
saleable IP

Urban growth corridors
Regional cities of 50k+ populations
Digital reach

Provider of
choice identifiable,
recognised brand

People
Risk
Our
Financial Sustainability
Service Innovation
Five Year Goals and Priorities
Partners
Intellectual Property
Geography
Customer Relevance

The arms are the goals or result areas (more on this in Part 2), and at the end of each one is a statement describing what that will look like. A business-focused human service organisation might have 'legs' on its spider for revenue, profitability or margins, service expansion, people capability, information and intellectual property, technology, and profile. You should identify legs by asking 'What's most important for us to show?' or 'What are the most important problems we have to solve as an organisation?'

If you draw the purpose and problems in the middle of the spider (its body), and each leg has a clear statement of where you want to be in two to three years, you can indicate on each leg how far along you are now. You can arrive at these statements by doing the following thought experiment. Imagine you are X years into the future, and then complete this sentence: When it comes to _____ (specify a particular leg, such as geography), we are an organisation that has recently _____ (in the case of geography, this might be 'expanded operations in urban growth corridors by forty per cent').

ACTION TO TAKE

If you're confident about forming your strategy, these are the questions you should ask yourself while you're forming it, to predict how well you'll internalise it:

Who did you involve? Who did you mark as your champions? How will you use them? Did you identify points of resistance? Who, and what?

1. Do you have a pivot point? Is there a single factor that will predict whether you can achieve your purpose?

2. In what do you need to invest so that you achieve your pivot point? Where are you putting your energies?

3. What's the simplest possible message you can deliver?

4. What are the changes required once your strategy goes live? Can you rank order them in terms of their effects on your people, or your people's readiness to lead or adopt them?

That brings us to the end of Part 1. By now, you know exactly what your everyday impact should be, and have taken steps to internalise a strategy in relation to that. In Part 2, I'll show you how to create everyday impact – every single day.

Part 2: Create everyday impact, every day

The problem: Nearly all public value organisations have a strategy. I know - I've seen them. Yet most organisations don't create the building blocks that allow them to execute their strategy. They don't give their people power to really own results that matter. They put disproportionate effort into things that don't truly matter. They accept yesterday's practices as sufficient for today - and tomorrow. And they do far more than they need to, in a misguided belief that it's what their customers want. To add insult to injury, a consequence of all this is that they're not seen the way they want to be seen. At best, they're misunderstood. At worst, they're maligned or criticised.

The solution: Everyday impact requires you to hand over control. First, control over results. These should be owned by your people, with light reporting burdens, and with clarity about how they create public value. Second, control over your customers. They can do far more for themselves than you give them credit for. Some might complain, but the majority will welcome your commitment to co-create with them. The best impact investment organisations can also prioritise ruthlessly, and opportunistically, and democratise innovation so that everyone has a role to play. Finally, they take back control by actively generating stories and data to create a narrative they want people to believe in.

There are six 'force-multipliers' that nearly all high-impact public value organisations I have observed and worked with have hardwired into their daily practice:

1. Care about results.
2. Focus on priorities.
3. Futureproof by innovating.
4. Leverage with partners and customers.
5. Complement your offering with likeminded entities.
6. Shamelessly build your profile.

In Chapters 7-12, I'll show you how to achieve and maintain all six of these things on a daily basis. Then in Chapter 13, I'll show you how to scale your best ideas, using the insights you've gained in the previous chapters. By the end of Part 2, you'll know exactly how to create everyday impact for your customers or beneficiaries, every single day.

CHAPTER 7:

Care about results

ANDREW'S OBSERVATION: Many organisations settle for less impact simply because they assume their people know what success looks like. But they don't test this. Nor do they report on it properly, there are no explicit positive consequences for achievement, and there are no obvious negative consequences for non-achievement. I also notice a tendency, especially at executive level, to make everyone responsible for everything. This means that, in truth, nobody is responsible. And, finally, I observe that there's too little attention being paid to doing the best consistently (consistently well and consistently efficiently).

The single reason why results matter is that impact is the consequence of results. One of my clients relies on bequests and other philanthropic contributions to provide it with between $2 million and $5 million of 'unconditional' revenue each year. They have two problems, however. First, that nobody 'owns' this result, so the result varies, sometimes dramatically. Second, there is no simple connection between the activity the philanthropy team carries out and their results each year. And, most importantly, they're measuring the wrong thing. They can tell you the gross revenues from bequests, but not the net result (after the costs of obtaining the bequests are factored in, and these are substantial). This faulty thinking means that this organisation is foregoing the biggest spur for improvement, which is a sense of progress towards goals[12].

---

12 A 2010 study by Harvard Business Review found the number one motivator among employees is a perception of making progress. This could be overcoming an obstacle, achievement of a milestone, or feedback on outcomes.

In this chapter, I'll show you how to create a sense of ownership around your results by helping you identify the right assurances for your organisation, and three key ingredients you must incorporate.

What assurances do you want?

One of my favourite restaurants in Bali is called Locavore (a locavore only eats what is obtained locally). The restaurant proudly states that apart from some of its alcohol, everything is produced by farmers and food producers from within a ten-kilometre radius. All the chefs, including co-founder Ray Adriansyah, even wear hats that read, 'Go local or go home'.

So, any starting point for ownership of results is the question: What do you want your people's hats to say? Or, to put it more seriously: What assurances do you want? I ask board members and executives this question even before I ask: What do you want to be accountable for? I find that focusing on assurance is a much more challenging and therefore valuable starting frame for directors because if their focus is initially on accountability, they will mentally delegate this, often rightly, to their chief executive. When I asked that question of IPC Health (one of the largest providers of community health services in my home state of Victoria), they said they wanted four assurances:

1. That we provide **care** that's *valued.*

2. That we have a *positive* **reputation**.

3. That we run an *effective* and *viable* **business**.

4. That we **operate** *soundly.*

To identify your 'hats' or assurances, I recommend the following process, which begins with identifying nouns and adjectives! First, go back to your purpose statement (see Chapter 1) and identify a small number of domains – these are your nouns. In IPC Health's case, they are care, reputation, business and operations. Then, pick punchy adjectives that sum up the assurance you want. Care that's *valued* was important to IPC Health because it had a history of client distrust and even criticism. A *viable* business was vital because it had a troubled financial history, from which it wanted to rapidly distance itself. Once you've agreed on these, essential follow-up questions for your strategists must include 'What does that mean?' or 'What would convince you of that?'

Three more must-have ingredients

At this point, you may be thinking, 'But Andrew, just being able to articulate these assurances doesn't ensure that people will do them!' That's very true. Ownership is maximised when we understand the behavioural psychology behind achievement in all types of organisations, not just public value organisations. Based on my experience, I believe that three further ingredients are needed:

1. **Logically linked activity.** People will own results that they can see arise from their, and others', actions.

2. **Intelligently minimal reporting.** At best, unnecessary reporting implies you don't know what you want. At worst, it implies you don't trust the people doing the work.

3. **Recognition.** Carefully considered rewards for those accountable for the results serve as motivation for future achievement.

Let's look at how exemplary agencies and non-profits do each of these.

1. LOGICALLY LINKED ACTIVITY

You can dramatically increase buy-in to your results when you can show your people one thing: How the activity they undertake contributes to measures of success against those results. This is known as a value chain.

A simple example of a value chain is a sanitation value chain, which the Bill & Melinda Gates Foundation use to guide funding to improve hygiene in developing countries. The foundation has invested $650 million over ten years to convert 'open defecation' areas into fully functioning sanitation value chains. The value here is that human waste is turned into other products with value, or is disposed of cleanly, by virtue of a chain of activity. Namely, capture, storage, transport and treatment.

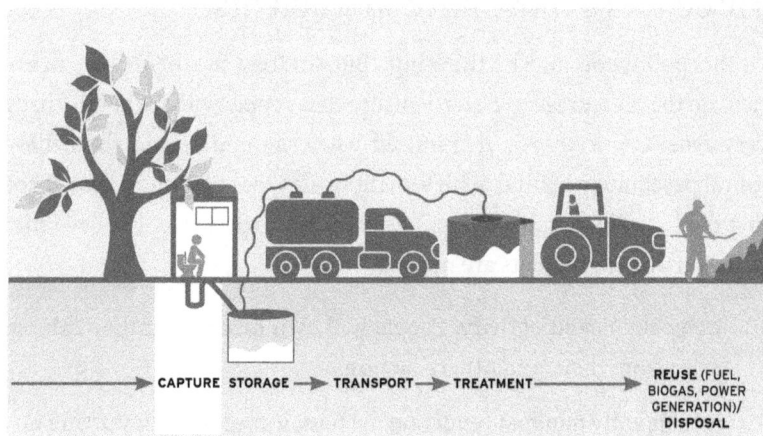

CAPTURE STORAGE ⟶ TRANSPORT⟶ TREATMENT ⟶ REUSE (FUEL, BIOGAS, POWER GENERATION)/ DISPOSAL

This is deceptively simple, and is worth breaking down into components:

- The primary **activity** we undertake ⟶ Capture
- **Success** we can measure ⟶ Waste stored and transported
- **Results** gained ⟶ Treatable waste
- **Impact** (purpose) ⟶ Safely disposed and reused waste

But what about instances where there isn't just a single, straight-line relationship between activity and results? Can you still achieve buy-in by making a very complex thing simpler? Yes, you can, and a good example is road safety in my home state of Victoria. We have a population of over five million and we are world leaders in the prevention of road deaths, having reduced deaths and serious injuries twelvefold since their peak in 1970. Ownership of these results is maximised when we tier the activities that lead to the desired results. If you look at the diagram overleaf, you can see an approach to measurement which classifies four powerful questions (displayed on the left-hand side) into logical levels that, in turn, drive different levels of detail in measurement. Each level answers a particular question:

1. What matters the most? Fewer road deaths. This sits at the top of the hierarchy, as the ultimate purpose or impact.

2. What works best? The evidence around road safety tells us that a combination of driver habits, road design and enforcement are optimum. These are the results that our interventions, or investments have brought about.

3. Where can we rationally invest? In just one area, driver habits, we can't invest in a driver-by-driver re-education and re-licensing program. But we can focus on two other major areas: The cars they drive, and their state of readiness or protection. So, we direct people towards the safest vehicles and we target specific categories of users who are more likely to die or be injured on the road.

4. Who or what would bring about the fastest, most positive result? We are likely to see results quickest if we build interventions[13] with young people, old people, motorcyclists and truck drivers.

13 You should aim for all interventions in your value chain to be evidence-based where possible. In my example above, motorcyclists are highlighted because of their propensity for accidents (much higher than cars), and interventions have known efficacy. For instance, putting anti-lock brakes (ABS) on motorcycles reduces fatalities and injuries by thirty-seven percent.

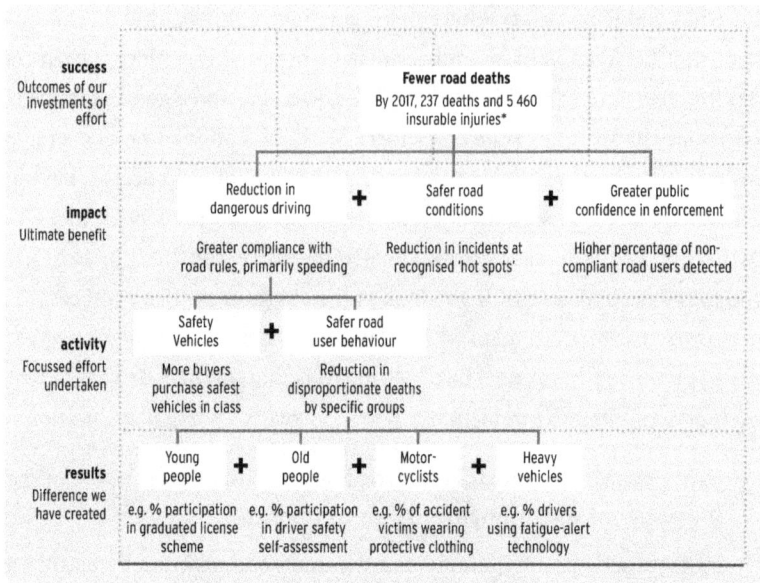

success
Outcomes of our investments of effort

Fewer road deaths
By 2017, 237 deaths and 5 460 insurable injuries*

impact
Ultimate benefit

Reduction in dangerous driving **+** Safer road conditions **+** Greater public confidence in enforcement

Greater compliance with road rules, primarily speeding | Reduction in incidents at recognised 'hot spots' | Higher percentage of non-compliant road users detected

activity
Focussed effort undertaken

Safety Vehicles **+** Safer road user behaviour

More buyers purchase safest vehicles in class | Reduction in disproportionate deaths by specific groups

results
Difference we have created

Young people **+** Old people **+** Motor-cyclists **+** Heavy vehicles

e.g. % participation in graduated license scheme | e.g. % participation in driver safety self-assessment | e.g. % of accident victims wearing protective clothing | e.g. % drivers using fatigue-alert technology

*Adapted from: Victoria's Road Safety Action Plan 2011 - 2012, p.5

The examples I've provided sum up the guidance that I give to my clients to help them work out the logical flows that exist between tiers of activity and results sought. Strip away anything superfluous, and don't make the mistake of wanting to include everything. Stick to the main features, and you'll achieve wonders in getting your people to understand and accept their role in your, and your clients', successes.

2. MINIMAL REPORTING

A local government client of mine had 174 indicators in its strategic plan. A public hospital reported on 212 items to its board across the year; typical board packs were six to eight centimetres thick! The dilemma here is easily seen: There is no indication of what's most important. Therefore, boards become reactive (to the latest crisis, or opportunity) or fragmented (by passion or area of expertise).

I've seen these scenarios become CEOs' nightmares, to the point where clients of mine have spent up to a quarter of their time 'managing' their board. Unfortunately, this happens not because someone decided that 174 or 212 were optimal numbers of reportables, but rather because, over time, more were added. Like a garage that gets filled up with once-useful stuff (hedge trimmers, toys, pet equipment, bike parts), public value organisations' reporting systems are often full of once-useful items that are no longer necessary. Like a garage spring clean, most organisations would benefit from a yearly check-up, where you ask yourself: Do we still need this?

To achieve a true minimal reporting system that provides all of the assurances you need, there are four questions you need to answer:

1. **What measure(s) would satisfy the assurance we're seeking?**

   So, if IPC Health is interested in measuring 'valued care', one of the measures of this would be the number of 'did not attends' (people who make appointments and don't show up). To measure efficacy of care, they track self-reported outcomes (where clients answer questions like 'Did your condition improve?' and then 'How likely is it that this was because of the care you received?') It's important to realise that you won't, in all cases, have a measurement system for everything, so you'll need to stage the development of more relevant measures over time.

2. **What's the appropriate form of the report?**

   Here is where minimalism really pays off. I differentiate between four types of reports, from most to least difficult to collect and report on:

   - **Narrative:** Interpretive text, written to help explain a result, or argue a case.
   - **List:** Dot points or checklist summaries of results, milestones or activities.

- **Quantitative:** Aggregated data (not raw) with a signalling system to aid framing (for example, lines to show where expectations are, or bands to show benchmarking ranges).

- **Exception:** Statements by responsible officers stating that all results are within previously discussed and approved boundaries (for example, many financial results and compliance reports).

You should start by assuming everything is an exception report, and then asking, successively up the scale, 'Would a quantitative report assure us?' If not, 'Would a list-based report assure us?' If not, 'Would a narrative report assure us?' If you want to see an example of a system such as this, go to http://www.workwell.com.au and look for the free resources.

3. Who owns each result?

This doesn't mean who does the work. It means creating an accountable owner for each and every measure. For instance, IPC Health captures 'did not attend' as an exception report, so if DNAs are less than that, there is no requirement to report. However, if, in a three-month period, there's a service area with fifteen per cent DNA, someone has to speak to it, help explore reasons for it, undertake to return it to the desired range, and then report back. In some cases, the 'owner' is a board subcommittee (for instance, on company investments, or on safety in a hospital) and, in rare cases, I'd allow the entire executive team to be accountable for a result area. But try to minimise this because, as I said earlier, when everyone is responsible, nobody is.

4. When do we need to know?

Last on your minimalism crusade is planning the most intelligently minimal cycles of reporting. Many organisations fall into the trap of assuming that either everything should be reported on the same cycle (such as monthly) or that data should be reported when it becomes available (for example, if client outcomes data is aggregated quarterly, that's when an organisation is most likely to filter it to the board).

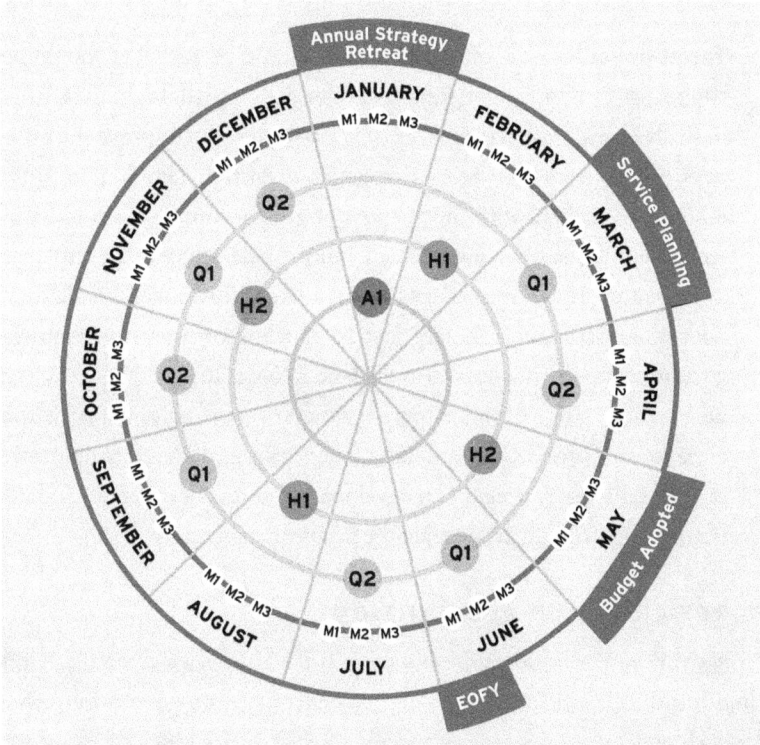

I suggest clients draw a circle, like a clock face, but representing a year with months around the perimeter. At twelve o'clock should be the organisation's annual strategy reset meeting, in whatever form that takes. Elsewhere should be noted critical dates for contract expiry, or budgeting against financial year, and so on. Inside the circle, on concentric layers, should be the reportables that occur:

- Annually (A1)
- Half-yearly (H1, H2)
- Quarterly (Q1, Q2)
- Monthly (M1, M2, M3)

The criterion for how often something should be reported should be two things taken together: Report as often as you get data about *changes* in the business, which enable *decisions* to be made to improve the business. For instance, New Story Housing is an entrepreneurial non-profit established in 2012 with the purpose of giving slum dwellers in Latin America a house they own, which can provide safety and consistency of tenure. They fund blocks of fifty, 100 or 200 houses. While each house's construction averages just $6,000, the organisation requires governments to provide titles to the land in order to give security to the new owners. None of this requires granular reporting to a board. The cycle for this process takes months, not weeks, and therefore quarterly or even half-yearly updates on development (a mix of exception, quantitative and list reports) provide the necessary assurance.

3. REWARDS AND RECOGNITION

Already, if you're building intelligently linked actives and results, and then building a minimalist reporting system, you've gone a long way towards getting your people connected to your desired results. However, both of those phases are only taking care of the destination planning, not the journey itself.

Sunbury Community Health built a system whereby all managers came together each quarter to look over the organisation's seventeen objectives and the measures for each. This is no 'tick and flick' exercise. They ask three sets of profound questions each time they meet:

- **Recognise:** Does the measure tell the whole story? What else do we need to know? Is there a better way of tracking this?

- **Celebrate:** Why is this worth celebrating? Who was responsible? How can we let them know we're impressed with the results?

- **Improve:** Why did we not succeed? Can we identify the root cause? Is this really the best we can do?

What most high-impact public value organisations do is build dashboard reporting systems. Sometimes these are quite simple (traffic light systems) while other systems are quite sophisticated, with backend data aggregation and real-time visibility of results occurring, especially where the organisation is working in highly dynamic environments (for example, shifting waitlists for time-critical services, or where a percentage difference in occupancy or utilisation makes a big difference to a financial result). The best such systems ensure six basic conditions are in place:

- **Need to know.** This means one size *doesn't* fit all. Does the marketing manager need to know about occupancy? Does the CFO need to know about IT system uptime?

- **Less is more.** Like I keep emphasising with goals, and with result areas, don't track something just because you can. Don't include it on the dashboard just because you've got some white space to fill and two people from HR have asked for it.

- **Refresh rates.** Highly dynamic dashboards don't need refreshing per se, as they are either 'always on' or have scheduled pop-ups. If your data is more strategic, and less operational, and is only refreshed weekly or monthly, then ensure you've got a notification system or a way that forces views and some kind of response or interaction.

- **Interact with it.** Average dashboards present information. Really good ones enable the user to interrogate, to drill down, to compare.

- **Design it.** Use the right data visualisation (not the same old bar chart for everything). Use an inverted pyramid (main points at the top, trends in the middle, and detail at the bottom). Use the five-second rule (the thing that the person most wants from a dashboard should be gleaned within five seconds).

- **Put the data in the hands of the user.** Put measurement in the hands of those doing the work, not an external compliance function. Otherwise, you have an internal 'policing', which can seem adversarial. If you think you need an audit process because of concerns about dishonesty, it's a signal that your measurement is used for the wrong purposes – it should be about demonstrating value and creating improvements. And finally, teach people how to use it. This means showing non-quantitative people the value of the numbers.

Frequently asked questions

There are three questions that my clients typically ask about results ownership:

1. **How do we get people really engaged with results, apart from just making them aware of results?**

   The best way by far is using the results to drive improvements. One of the main questions I ask my clients about their reporting is: How does knowing this help you become better? One client told me, 'We're very proud that our client satisfaction survey scores have been above ninety-five per cent for the past three years.' I asked him two questions:

   - How does this help you improve?

- If it dropped to ninety-four per cent, what would you do differently? What about ninety-one per cent?

- He didn't have clear answers to either question. I observed that he'd do better to have a result area that was 'improvements arising from client feedback'. He should then relegate client satisfaction to a 'hygiene factor' that is reported by exception (that is, assume that satisfaction is high, and only report on it if it drops below a certain threshold).

2. **What do public value organisations most commonly overlook when it comes to accountability for results?**

Consistency. It's a boring answer, but it's true. This is something that the best private value providers do very well. Southwest Airlines turns around planes at gates within fifteen minutes, consistently. Amazon delivers parcels in its core locations, same day or next day, consistently. Apple's supply chain gets goods into its stores on their scheduled release dates. Results ownership is about standards, and so when standards are not met, these types of businesses routinely ask: What stopped us doing it properly?

3. **Isn't ownership really about power? If we make someone responsible for a result, don't we have to give him or her the powers to achieve it, and to remedy a poor result?**

Yes. I once helped an organisation where the chief executive would spend an hour pointing out missed deadlines, unimpressive results, and so on. He'd end his meetings with, 'I'm deeply disappointed.' Then he'd stalk out, leaving the executives to sigh and grumble among themselves. However, every notable decision was made by him. Every new initiative was approved by him. Every hire above a certain level was to be authorised by him. Every policy document was held onto by him, and gone over with a red pen before it was returned to its author. This was a case where results were poor because results ownership was non-existent, because there were no clear decision rights. In other words, there was no clear set of delegations for decision making.

There are many ways to arrive at decision rights, but they are all based on a simple concept once an organisation has set the fundamentals of identity (purpose, role and values) and focus (goals and activities). A decision inventory can then be created, which answers the following questions:

- Who is responsible for organisational structures?
- Who is responsible for evaluation of program X?
- Who is responsible for designing criteria before service Y goes out to tender?

These can be plugged into a hierarchy (with the board at the top, senior managers in the middle, leaders near the bottom, and the inclusion of consultative bodies, client inputs, and so on). The key to setting good decision rights is devolution (the lowest level possible, or the level whom the decision affects the most, makes the decisions) and transparency (ensuring that both up and down the hierarchy, those that need to be involved can be).

ACTION TO TAKE

You've got this far, so well done, as this is a critical chapter in this book. Organisations who get everything thus far right (purpose, role, values, and then scale and goals), but don't get this right, wonder why nothing changes despite having a great strategy. That is because despite the strategic internalisation that you may have done (discussed in Chapter 6), there is no sustainable way for people to remain engaged and focused. So, check on the following:

1. Can you clearly link action to desired results? Does your thinking withstand critical scrutiny of experts and pass the 'it's obvious' test? This test is simply asking: Does it make sense that if we do A and B, we get C? If it doesn't, you've overcomplicated your value chain.

2. Don't measure what you can - measure what you want. Quantity of measures is proportional with meaninglessness. Not all results are equal. That doesn't mean getting rid of some results, but simply demoting them. Ultimately, all metrics should inform decision making.

3. Ensure your people are recognised for great results. That will only happen when clear owners are identified for each result area.

CHAPTER 8:

Focus on priorities

ANDREW'S OBSERVATION: Many public value organisations don't have a deliberate process for prioritisation. They accumulate services, products, operations and staff. Deciding what to keep and what to let go is relegated to the too-hard basket. Externally, the same confusion occurs in knowing which opportunities to go for, and which to let go.

How often do you have to make a decision? If you're a senior leader in a public value organisation, I'm guessing you make dozens of decisions every single day. Decisions about money, staff, clients or customers. And, when that's done, more decisions on programs, policies, politics and profile.

Perhaps you're thinking, 'Decisions are the reason I'm employed. My organisation employed me for my judgement, my ability to assess best courses of action among alternatives, and to see clarity in chaos and confusion.' That is of course true, and the key to good decision making is the ability to prioritise. In fact, after strategy formation, the most common request I receive as a consultant is: 'Andrew, we need help prioritising.' In this chapter, I'll show you how to do exactly that, using a couple of proven methods.

Hitting the sweet spot of investment

The most successful public value organisations have extremely well-honed and targeted frameworks that act as guidelines for decision making and prioritising. For instance, the Institute for Healthcare Improvement (IHI) has developed what it calls its twelve interventions. These are the twelve issues on which thousands of participating hospitals are asked to campaign, and have been proved to reduce fatalities. Here are some examples:

- Deploying rapid response teams.
- Preventing central line bloodstream infections.
- Preventing pressure ulcers.
- Reducing surgical complications.
- Preventing adverse drug events through medical reconciliation.

What this means is that when IHI has to assess its priorities (for instance, whether to support a campaign in hospital X in state Y), it has a readymade guideline for this. In other words, the question simply becomes: Which of these twelve campaigns does hospital X wish to subscribe to? It's a little like what a restaurant does by creating a menu, which reduces every potential choice and priority to twenty items that are within the kitchen's capabilities, budget and timeframes.

Such guidelines can help you answer this question: What should (or shouldn't) we do? They can also help you answer a second question: How much of something should we do (or not do)? There's a fine line between doing too much and not doing enough. You have to find it. To do this, I have found a very useful guideline is the law of diminishing returns. I'm sure you've experienced it. Whether it's alcohol, shopping, eating, or hi-fi equipment, the rule is the same: There's a point at which further investment is not worth the gain. This is called satiation. We're incapable of taking any more in. The first effective human study of this was in agriculture. People thought that their crop yield was strictly related to how many seeds they planted. Every six seeds yielded about five plants. If you planted twelve seeds, would you get ten plants? What if you planted twenty-four seeds, or thirty-six? You might get more plants, but only if they were far enough apart, as they're competing for moisture and light if they're too close together. This process is called optimisation.

To apply this guideline to a real-world public value scenario, imagine a city government with an old, crumbling community swimming pool. The city could spend $5 million refurbishing it, only to now have an old pool which has been patched up. The state government then offers $12 million to build a new pool. But this creates a problem: Is $12 million enough?

The dilemma is that we don't know what the pool is worth. If we were calculating it on a private value investment basis, we could factor in cost of capital, lifespan cost and revenue streams, and arrive at either a breakeven or profit position. Job done. But, with public value, we don't know what it's worth. Will a $12 million pool just as effectively achieve its social objectives as a $60 million pool? Let's say the objective is community endorsement, whereby people say things like 'We've got a great leisure facility in our community' or 'We would re-elect the people who built the pool.' If you spend nothing, you get zero people saying these things. If you spent $5 million doing the refurbishment, you'd get a small number, but not many. If you spent $12 million, you'd get more, but you wouldn't get five times as many if you spent $60 million. The increment ends up as a curve, not a straight line, as illustrated in this diagram. I refer to this as the Investment Sweet Spot.

OUTCOME

COULD
SPEND

Sweet
spot

MUST
SPEND

Criticised for
spending too little

Criticised for
spending too much

INVESTMENT

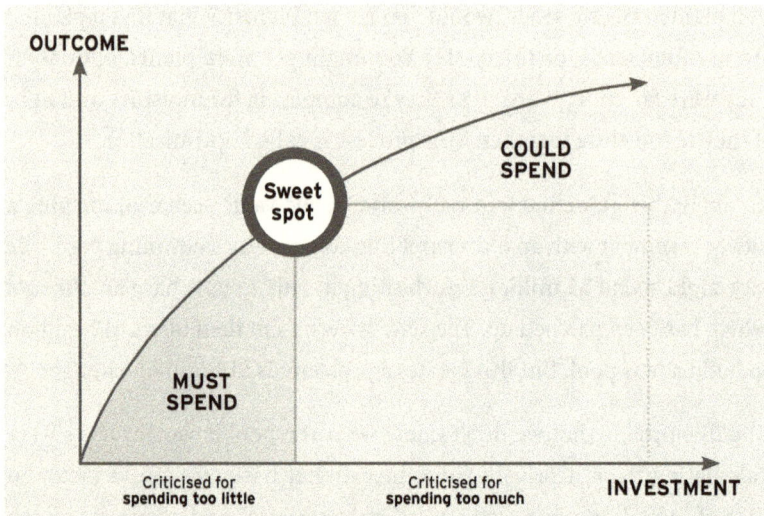

Someone's got to draw that value curve, or at least estimate it, so that you can place a big dot on the point where the curve shifts its angle from going up to going sideways. That's the sweet spot.

This is less mathematical than a careful assessment of sentiment, so my advice on how to plot that sweet spot is to agree on the balance between three factors:

1. DESIRE

What do your end users want the most? What do they want the least? You need ways of investigating what handful of things your constituency wants you to be outstanding on, and on what they merely want the basics delivered. One way to do this is by running focus groups where people have to force-rank a list of options, or have forced choice between alternatives ('If you could have either A or B, but not both, which would you choose?'). Another excellent way to do this is to ask people to allocate resources ('You have $100 to spend on X initiatives. Allocate the dollars in proportion with what you think is important').

2. SATIATION

To be sated is to be full. Anything extra we'd consume beyond this point is worth less. My local library has all the bells and whistles: Reading areas, rentable office space, children's play area, video games, work stations, research advisers, a rooftop garden and picnic area. Oh yes, and books. It's stunning. The first time I visited, I stayed for hours, enjoying all of this. The second time, just a half hour. Now, I just drop in and out quickly to do what I need to do. I am satiated. Each type of project will have its own pattern of economic satiation.

Some are not worth doing cheaply (like a library), while others can be scaled from very small seeds indeed. If so, the concept of the minimum viable product is highly valuable. This is the ability to develop, at lowest cost, an example of the feature set which satisfies the bare minimum use requirement. This enables market testing to occur and allows you to gain feedback for further product development. As an example, a disability support organisation might offer a weekly supported outing at a fixed time as a way of testing a market for social supports. Eventually, the product might be a fully-fledged social support service that is configurable or selectable by its users. This makes satiation much easier to track: You can stop adding features once your customer's basic needs are satisfied.

3. OPPORTUNITY COST

What is rendered unaffordable by each increase? This is the ability to sequence investments, so that if a local government invests several million dollars in a pool, it'll be unable to invest $500,000 in an Uber app-like garbage pick-up service, or $1 million into a feasibility study for self-driving rubbish trucks, until a later date.

If you plot the dot on the value curve correctly, you will have two distinct segments underneath your curve either side of the dot. Below and to the left of the dot is the 'must spend' area. This is what your community, constituents or users expect you to spend, as their satisfaction (however you measure it) increases disproportionately with each dollar you spend. In the case of the swimming pool example, this refers to the $5 million refurbishment. Above and to the right of the dot is the 'could spend' area. This is optional spending, which satisfies some needs, but is beyond the point of satiation for most of your users. In the swimming pool example, this would be a brand new swimming pool costing upwards of $12 million. If you are a publicly accountable body and you miscalculate in either direction, you'll attract the attention of the tabloid press ('We are being deprived!' or 'Wasteful spending by government!') It's therefore crucial that you hit the sweet spot of investment as much as possible.

Another factor that ties public value organisations into knots is their inability to predict the future. That's why I encourage my clients to develop testable assumptions, which were discussed in Chapter 6. For a local government, for example, relevant testable assumptions might be that people will almost entirely expect service delivery to be booked, tracked and received via mobile devices, that density will spike dramatically in certain areas, and that consumers are increasingly willing to pay for differentiated services. If you collect evidence for these testable assumptions, and revisit them every year or two, then you can act as if they are true, and this will dramatically aid focus and prioritisation.

Fighting opportunity gluttony

Most of my clients complain that there are *too many* opportunities for them to invest in. One community health client estimates that she could bid for two to three new service initiatives *per month*, averaged across the year.

Another, involved in early childhood services, says that every week her organisation is invited to 'take over' an underperforming childcare centre. Still another has said that she and her board had to consider no fewer than three merger invitations (initiated by other parties) within a twelve-month period. This is true opportunity gluttony, where these organisations are presented with far more than they can (and should) invest in.

So, how can you determine which opportunities are the golden eggs, and which are merely distractions, or even damaging? There are two ways to consider prioritisation of opportunities. The first is against a *market filter*, and the second is against an *execution filter*. In other words, you must first ask: Is this viable? (Should we do this?) and then ask: Is this possible? (Can we do this?) The market filtering I often use with my clients looks like this:

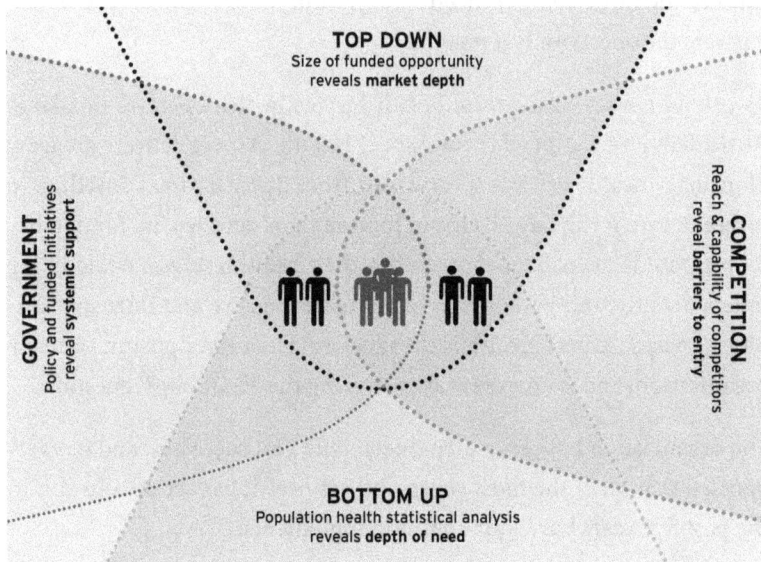

TOP DOWN
Size of funded opportunity
reveals **market depth**

GOVERNMENT
Policy and funded initiatives
reveal systemic support

COMPETITION
Reach & capability of competitors
reveal barriers to entry

BOTTOM UP
Population health statistical analysis
reveals **depth of need**

This enables a public value organisation to rapidly assess an opportunity by determining if a viable market exists for a proposed service within a known location. The following factors require analysis concurrently:

1. **Analysis of need** (bottom up): Do people need it? How many people have this need?

2. **Size of funded market** (top down): Is there a revenue model for it?

3. **Government: Does government support it?** (At the very least, there should be no policy or regulatory impediments to it.)

4. **Competition:** Is the competition modest, weak or even absent?

Let's say the opportunity you're considering ticks all four boxes. The opportunity sounds good on paper, but that doesn't mean you should venture forward. You still need to carry out an execution filter, which answers the question: Is it possible?

I work with a very successful health service, which operates in a large Australian city. Let's call them Aspect Health. Aspect delivers an array of primary health services (everything from dentistry to counselling to in-home care for the aged) through more than ten sites. Its fundamental purpose is to enable people to live their healthiest lives while living independently, and without having to use expensive and intrusive hospital services. Aspect Health is the ideal model of an opportunity-ready organisation, and is an expert at answering the 'Could we?' question.

The organisation has reverse-engineered its past successes, and has recognised that *all* of the most successful services it has set up and run in the past five years have four common ingredients:

- **Presence:** 'Our service offer is strengthened in a particular market (a geographic area, service type or customer type).'

- **Significance:** 'Our repute is strengthened among customers, collaborators, community stakeholders, and funders or investors.'
- **Innovation:** 'The service design enables us to disrupt, or anticipate disruptions.'
- **Capacity:** 'We can deliver within the resources available to us.'

These become 'gates' to assess the practicality of opportunities. In other words, every opportunity is 'pushed through the funnel' and assessed against each of these criteria. Aspect has done three additional things to enable this to occur:

- **Specify:** Each of the ingredients has required between three and eight further elements. For instance, innovation consists of the following:
  - The design of the service is innovative.
  - The service can start small and can then scale.
  - The project has a passionate lead (a person who believes in it).

  Once again, these elements were arrived at by asking: When have we been successful in the past? One of their most successful counselling services had an innovative design (it relied partially on text message coaching), which was rolled out to a very limited audience at first (recall the notion of minimum viable products from earlier in the chapter), and was led by an internal evangelist who strongly believed in the model.

- **Rate:** For each element, a rating system was developed. Simple Likert scales work very well, where zero indicates no rating (in other words, there is nothing innovative about the service design) and a score of five is high (this indicates a significant departure from usual practice).

- **Assess:** Each opportunity was assessed by a minimum of three managers or executives, including the executive whose area the proposed opportunity would fall within.

The consequences of this approach were as you might expect. Far less time is spent on unrealistic opportunities because they are filtered out early. The diagram below shows how this works, by plotting the benefits score against the risks score. Bottom right (high risk, low benefit) is clearly not for consideration, top left (high benefit, low risk) is.

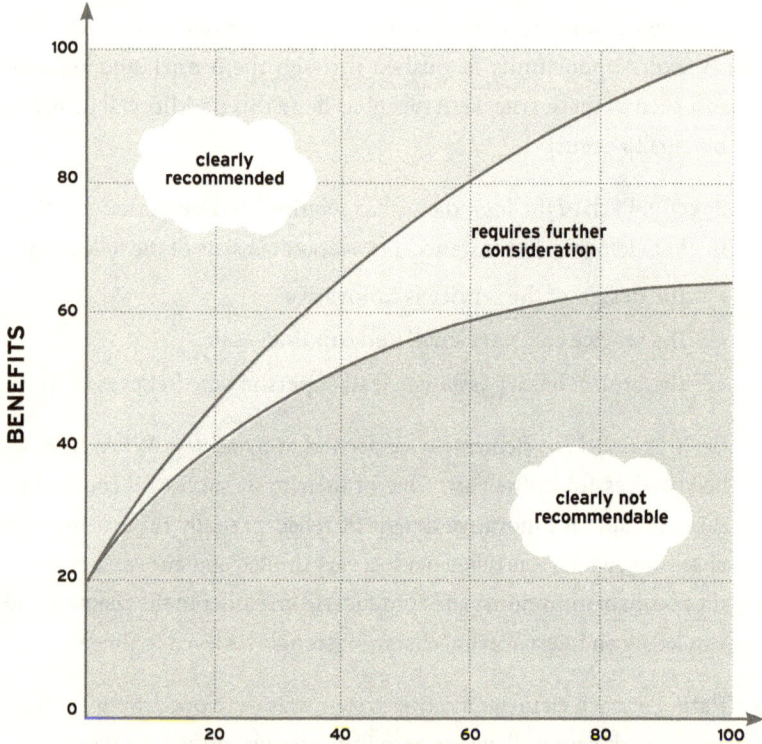

And there is far less 'regret focus' after an idea is discarded ('You know, I still think that if we had have done X...'). Remember that the scores aren't real! They are simply there as a heuristic – a loose set of rules that create decision-making shortcuts and allow a group of people to accelerate learning. Consequently, you should focus your discussion not on the scores themselves, but on any criteria where raters disagreed. You can then develop your business cases by bolstering the lowest-scoring elements. What Aspect has done very well is remembering that this execution filter is not a quantitative assessment task for its own end, but exists solely for the purpose of ensuring group agreement on where Aspect needs to focus its efforts.

Frequently asked questions

There are three questions that I'm frequently asked about prioritisation and opportunities:

1. **How does risk relate to prioritisation?**

    Risk is merely the flipside of opportunity. Opportunity answers the question 'What could we do differently or better?', while risk answers the question 'What could stop us?' In public value organisations, risk is often treated as if it is a concept of its own, so we have risk frameworks, risk committees, risk managers, and so on. Risk is the business of everyone who is responsible for opportunity, so why don't we have opportunity frameworks (which include risks), opportunity committees (which consider risks) and opportunity managers (who assess risks)?

2. **Should we go in search of opportunities, or merely respond to them?**

    This depends on your strategy, but as I have a bias to action, I'd say, 'Go to them before they come to you,' or, even better, 'Go to them before you become ineffective or irrelevant.' The most successful organisations I work with do routine environmental scans that involve service and product development opportunities, partnership (and acquisition and merger) opportunities, and capability development opportunities. So, have a pipeline for both inbound and outbound opportunities, and ensure you're 'response ready' when opportunities arise. You may do this by using testable assumptions in quarterly discussions that aim to identify opportunities by developing alternate strategic scenarios, or by scheduling regular foresight sessions for the board and executive team.

One of my clients has estimated that they have less than thirty days to prepare a response to service expansion opportunities and, consequently, they have built templates that enable them to rapidly put together market assessments and partner assessments, as well as descriptors for their purpose and role and strong capability statements. Remember that opportunity assessment is a muscle. With practice, you'll gain both reaction time and strength, and, as a result, be much fitter for the big opportunities when they present themselves.

3. **What if a decision isn't a simple yes or no?**

Very often this is the case, whereby a priority isn't a matter of 'Should we or shouldn't we?' but 'How much should we?' or 'When should we?' or 'With whom should we?' In these cases, I advise my clients to build in options thinking, or tiers or stages of investment. 'Option Zero' simply retains the status quo and costs nothing (although the downstream cost might be higher than zero). Beyond Option Zero, you can construct a series of plausible options. These might be financially based (invest $200,000, $500,000 or $2 million), geographically based (expand into area A, A and B, or B and C), or relate to the scope of the project (initiate a limited, full or enhanced service offer). In addition, you can also ask whether it is feasible to respond to an opportunity by deliberately not meeting all needs, but simply those most central, for the purposes of testing viability or capability.

ACTION TO TAKE

Senior leaders are paid to create contexts and systems in which the best decisions can be made. To do this, think about:

1. Decision making as a highly dynamic, not fixed, capability. Unless you're a highly capital-intensive business (like an affordable housing agency), your opportunities come and go quickly.

2. Your categories, criteria, diminishing returns and testable assumptions.

3. Which reactive and proactive opportunities have you seriously considered recently, currently, and in the immediate future?

4. Identify market filters and execution filters, based on your organisation's past successes, or the successes of other exemplars.

CHAPTER 9:

Futureproof by innovating

ANDREW'S OBSERVATION: Public value organisations that remain stuck in the bureaucratic model are too willing to settle for what they've always done, and how they've always done it. It's often not because of lack of will – it's because they haven't yet found quick, effective ways to bring ideas to life, with a minimum of friction and stalling, and a maximum of energy and rapid melding.

How do the best organisations turn the thoughts in one person's head into the actions of many?

Many of the world's most successful enterprises recognise that innovation is the single biggest predictor of sustainable success. A 2011 survey by PwC of 1,200 CEOs from around the world found that innovation, along with increasing their existing business, outstrips all other means of potential expansion, including moving into new markets, mergers and acquisitions, and joint ventures and other alliances. Furthermore, putting this into the hands of as many people as possible is key, yet the same study concluded that middle managers are not natural allies of innovation, as they reject new ideas in favour of efficiency. In this chapter, I'll reveal how you can democratise innovation, and innovate 'on demand' for the benefit of your staff, your customers, and your organisation as a whole.

Democratising innovation

The democratisation of innovation challenges a lot of top-down leaders, but a good example can be found in Facebook, which recognised that the typical hierarchical system of permission-based innovation was slow and punitive. Think about how this typically works:

A manager has an idea. She takes it to her director. They agree it has merit. A paper is prepared and presented to a committee, steering group or senior team. They consider it. More information is needed. The manager provides it. The idea is approved. The manager is notified. She now has permission to proceed with a timeframe, a budget, and a set of expectations to prove. Whether she succeeds or not, a report has to be provided back up the chain. If the idea is successful, then the real work begins of how to internalise the newfound revelation.

Phew. I'm exhausted just thinking about it, but I'm sure you've participated in similar bureaucratic processes. Is there an alternative way, which streamlines people's motivation to innovate and removes the friction or blockers? Yes, there is. Facebook has short-circuited this process with two simple realisations:

- Innovation is a necessity, not an option. Therefore, no permission is required. Rather, there is an expectation that everyone does it.

- Put as few obstacles in the path of innovators as possible, including *no* expectation of success.

Facebook has created a truly experimental culture by using this system instead:

A developer has an idea. Like all Facebook developers, she has the ability to partition some users (typically 50,000 or 100,000) for her experiment. She modifies the Facebook platform for her cohort, and then observes user behaviour. She knows the results on which success is judged, and they're always the same: Time spent on the platform, connections formed and used, revenue created and user satisfaction. She notes the results. If they're not acceptable, she resets the cohort to default and tries something else. If the results are great, she makes a report recommending inclusion of the change into the core platform. She has only one rule: Don't break the platform. Apart from this one rule, freedom to explore is not only permitted – it is expected.

This democratisation of innovation means that in any given month, all Facebook developers are innovators, but also that anyone who uses Facebook is probably an experimental subject. This means that trialling and testing is not linear – it's opportunistic. It's not plan-based – it's energy-based. Like my son is judged at school on effort more than results, you should be allocating resource to experimentation that stimulates that effort. Importantly, those resources are often not financial. In other words, you don't need a research team, a special building or a development fund. Instead, like Facebook, what you need are these three keys to democratised innovation:

- **Expectations.** Facebook assumes that all engineers will innovate; publishes case studies and guidance of prior successes; convenes peer groups to discuss wins and fails; and, of course, has leaders consistently prompting engineers.

- **Process.** Facebook's methodology provides the lowest barrier to experimentation but still ensures the 'platform doesn't break'.

- **Integration.** Facebook offers an easy way to get positive improvements authorised and integrated into the core platform.

Innovating on demand

The likes of Facebook and Amazon stand out because they can *innovate on demand*. In other words, they apply creative processes to business and customer problems, and do this repeatedly with high success rates.

An early star of such an approach was Walt Disney. Disney's achievement was to create an unparalleled string of commercially successful *and* creatively successful animated movies, starting with Mickey Mouse in the 1930s and continuing right up to Disney's death in 1966.

Over his lifetime, Disney produced some 680 films (mostly short animations) and nineteen full-length animated feature films. The vast majority of these were both creative and commercial successes. This is no coincidence. Disney organised his work so that it guaranteed creative, innovative outcomes. His revolutionary approach kept his staff focused in their thinking and design of a particular project. So, how did he do it with such consistent results?

Disney's approach involved three rooms:

1. **The Dreamers' Lounge.** This was a comfortable room where ideas were spun, dreams were harvested, no concept was too crazy, and ridiculous hunches and inspirations were laughed about and followed through.

2. **The Realists' Workshop.** The 'dreams' from the first room were coordinated, and storyboards (another Disney innovation) were created. These storyboards placed characters and events into a sequence. Some worked, but the majority bombed.

3. **The Critics' Cupboard.** At first, this was literally a small room under a staircase, where the whole crew would offer a no-holds-barred critique of the work that came from the Realists' Workshop. It's important to note that it was always the work that was criticised, never the individual.

If a work survived the Critics' Cupboard, it was ready for production. If it didn't, it went back to the Dreamers' Lounge for further work. The key, Disney found, was to allow each of these processes to occur in their own time and space, and, sometimes, with their own people who specialised in each form of thinking. You can use the Disney model to:

- *Invest* in a venture or business.
- *Answer* a question.
- *Build* something.
- *Introduce* a product or service.
- *Extend* markets or segments.
- *Grow* capabilities or skills.
- *Create* a service or product design.
- *Integrate* a complex system.
- *Transform* a set of beliefs or an organisation's culture.

Frequently asked questions

At this point, my clients typically come to me with two questions:

1. **What if our people just don't think creatively?**

    You have to train them. More accurately, you have to train them out of what is known as functional fixedness. Functional fixedness is a mental block that prevents you from using an object in a new way to solve a problem. For example, if you need a paperweight but you only have a hammer, functional fixedness is when you can only see the hammer as something for pounding nails with, not holding down papers.

    There are two chief ways I train people out of functional fixedness:

    - **'De-fixate' my instructions:** You can deliberately ask people to come up with *as many ways as possible* to achieve an outcome. Or ask them *what not to use*. (For example, 'Do this without assuming you have access to existing staff, processes, software or tools.') Or ask them to *presume a blank slate* or green field. (For example, 'If you were building this from scratch …') Recently, I worked with six local governments who de-fixated by asking themselves, 'What would our services to the region look like if we had no local government boundaries?' Of course, this is not realistic or probable, but it immediately freed up thinking and led to numerous creative options that *are* realistic.

- **Overcome prototypes:** Unlike children, adults take hundreds of mental shortcuts daily by categorising objects by single use. We see a spoon and immediately label it as a tool for eating (not a lever, or a scoop, or a drumstick, or a projectile). We see a Support Officer Level C and immediately see a tool for providing an agreed level of client support (not as a person who could educate clients, or provide business insights, or evaluate an intervention, or analyse data). To overcome such prototypic thinking, I ask people to mentally break down the object (or role, or department, or process) into its components. Then, we can ask: What could these components be used for? Similarly, by putting unfamiliar prototypes together, you can stimulate people to overcome the prototypes. (For example, 'How would you use a spoon, a candle, some thumbtacks and matches to get out of a locked room?')

2. **Why don't our meetings result in much innovative thinking?**

Because you're used to planning. I would predict that most of your group encounters are one of two types of meetings. Either it's an information meeting, where the attendees' role is to listen and understand, or it's a planning meeting, where the expectation is to form action steps towards a known outcome as quickly as possible. If you truly want to generate more innovative thinking, you must help your people develop and hone four critical skills:

- **Problem-finding:** The successful leaders of the twenty-first century, be they designers or politicians or managers, need to do more than properly define important problems. They need to lead problem-finding, which means identifying such problems first, and then motivating others to try to solve them. All public value organisations, I believe, are fundamentally in the business of solving problems, so problem-finding should be an indispensable capability.

- **Argumentation:** There's a prevalent myth in many humanistic public value organisations that conflict is bad. But only emotional conflict is bad (if it's not resolved), whereas cognitive conflict is good. Cognitive conflict, also known as dissonance, can be broadly defined as the mental discomfort produced when someone is confronted with new information that contradicts their prior beliefs and ideas. This helps you eliminate groupthink (more on that later) and open up strategic possibilities.

- **Multiple perspectives:** Be willing to entertain more than one point of view about a problem. What helps is to have patience with other people's learning styles and process needs, including a commitment to casting the widest possible net to ensure diversity of ideas. Most challenging for some is that this then requires listening deeply and intelligently to points of view which seem strange, wrong, or just plain confused.

- **Deferring judgement:** Be willing to suspend certainty that you know what 'the answer' is, and, ultimately, be willing to be wrong and to learn in public.

ACTION TO TAKE

This is deceptive territory. Everyone wants to be innovative, but few are. Test your willingness by checking how well you invest time, money and effort into helping your staff routinely develop actionable insights.

1. Which groups or teams are successfully innovating? When and how often? What are their products? How do we use those products?

2. What problems can we identify? What's broken? What does 'impossible to possible' look like?

3. Where does our 'dreaming' happen? How do we de-fixate functionally? Who are our stars at assessing and promoting our ability to think well?

CHAPTER 10:

Leverage your customers

ANDREW'S OBSERVATION: Many public value organisations are not fully aware of the ability they have to use others' powers. They don't fully explore their leverage power, or their ability to intermediate. And, even when they're firmly involved in service delivery, they do not leverage the greatest power they have daily access to: Their customers' self-determination.

Jay is seventeen years old. He's a typical kid, living with his family in a tree-lined suburban street. He likes skateboarding, video games and bushwalking. He has a few close mates he's known since early childhood and has had a couple of girlfriends. But for a couple of years, he's been increasingly troubled with paranoid thoughts, hearing voices while in class at school, and has struggled to remember homework. He has distanced himself from his friends, and often won't leave the house. His parents are very worried about him, and his teachers have recommended he see a psychologist.

It turns out Jay has early onset psychosis, and he is put in the care of a psychiatrist and psychologist to manage his hallucinations and disordered thinking. Traditionally, Jay might oscillate between being an inpatient (very costly and labour-intensive) and an outpatient (less costly), depending on the severity of his condition at any given time. However, what was impossible in the year 2000 is very possible today. Jay can prevent relapse through a next-generation social media-based tool. The artificial intelligence-assisted online platform Jay uses is called MOST (its four elements are described in the following diagram). It is based on positive psychology, was co-designed by young people, and combines peer support through moderated forums with therapy.

Moderated Online Social Therapy

mosl

01 SOCIAL NETWORKING AND THE CAFE

A Facebook-style newsfeed where users can contribute posts and comments, share experiences, give and obtain support, and gain perspectives and validation. Additional features include a Job Zone for vocational opportunities and information and Team Up, where users can set a challenge for themselves that others can then also participate in or follow as part of a 'cheer squad.'

TAKE A STEP 02

Steps are interactive therapy modules designed to exercise and develop a range of psychological skills. Therapy is delivered via engaging content that has been developed collaboratively by clinical psychologists, professional creative writers, leading comic developers and young people. Social interaction is embedded within steps through Talking Points, which are questions that promote users to discuss and share their own experiences.

03 TALK IT OUT

A space where users can nominate problems or difficulties they would like some help with to discuss in moderated groups following an evidence-based social problem solving framework. Once a user has nominated a problem and framed it together with a moderator, solutions are proposed and discussed by the users before a moderator wraps up the thread with a synopsis.

DO IT! (ACTIONS) 04

Users can access and 'do' specific behavioural experiments or tasks (referred to as "actions") to apply mindfulness, self-compassion, and personal strengths in real-world situations relevant to the young person (e.g., social context, school, work, alone, etc.).

From D'Alfonso Simon, Santesteban-Echarri Olga, Rice Simon, Wadley Greg, Lederman Reeva, Miles Christopher, Gleeson John, Alvarez-Jimenez Mario (2017) Artificial Intelligence-Assisted Online Social Therapy for Youth Mental Health, Frontiers in Psychology, Vol 8, p. 796.

Why is this such a significant development? Because it is unclear if benefits from early interventions can be sustained over time, and longer-term interventions may be required to maintain early clinical gains. However, in cases such as Jay's, due to the high intensity of face-to-face early intervention treatments, this may not be feasible. Therefore, thinking of internet-based interventions not as the sole form of intervention, but as an adjunct, may provide a cost-effective – and engaging – alternative that prevents loss of benefits.

However, until now, even online interventions have relied on human moderators to deliver therapeutic content, and so the inventors of the MOST platform are developing it further by using artificial intelligence

(AI) to offer suggestions to young people. In much the same way that Amazon offers recommendations, MOST will say, 'You may also be interested in X'. A further AI approach is similar to the way Facebook or Twitter places advertisements against related content. MOST will 'read' newsfeeds and place therapy suggestions alongside these. So far, both of these methods have proved strikingly effective.

While this example is specific to mental health interventions for young people, the general principles of 'do it differently' and 'do more with less' can apply to virtually any area of public value, from cleaning up contaminated sites to rehousing unwanted pets to developing parenting skills. Instead of relying on expensive professionals (environmental scientists, veterinarians, psychologists, and so on) for delivery, find ways of leveraging their expertise by transferring it, and multiplying it, among users, clients, patients or customers.

In this chapter, I'll show you how to gain power through leverage (using a successful case study as inspiration), and how to transfer power to your customers or beneficiaries.

Gaining power through leverage

Infoxchange is a non-profit social enterprise that uses technology to 'tackle the biggest social changes of our time'. Its purpose is simple: Digital inclusion – for everyone. Recognising that eighty-five per cent of homeless people in Australia use a smartphone prompted the organisation to build Ask Izzy, a mobile site which connects any person in a crisis with the organisations and services he or she needs most. So far, 350,000 people are using Ask Izzy, and not just homeless people, but a wide variety of people who are struggling to make their way in the world.

The secret to its success? Infoxchange works with 6,500 social justice organisations, which do the true heavy lifting of providing services to homeless people, people with disabilities or mental illnesses, and newly arrived refugees. But Infoxchange does the back-of-house heavy lifting, including client and case management systems, service coordination tools, community service directories, IT strategy and planning, cloud services, IT support and infrastructure, and project management. These are the necessary engines without which the entire machine would collapse.

Infoxchange realised in its infancy that a yawning gap existed in the CSO (community service organisation) and NGO (non-governmental organisation) sector. That is, a need to coordinate, organise and professionalise the data, and the informational and technological needs of these organisations. Because leverage is its currency, Infoxchange could never exist by itself, since its primary role is as an intermediary, but that is precisely why it is so necessary.

In short, there are four key principles Infoxchange embodies:

1. **Relevance.** The agencies Infoxchange works with are hugely supportive, even passionate, about the work it does.

2. **Utilisation.** Infoxchange is abundantly clear that its beneficiaries are the leaders of the work it does and that it seeks to amplify their capabilities, not replace them.

3. **Expertise.** Infoxchange applies its expertise judiciously, restricting it to areas that others do not have as core expertise, or where it is uneconomic or inefficient for them to do so.

4. **Ecosystems.** Infoxchange builds platforms, not products. In this way, the intellectual property created benefits the entire system, *and* enables the system to work better as a whole.

These four principles apply to many forms of public value organisations, be they regulators, community development organisations, advocacy bodies, or even specialist service providers. You can apply these principles quite easily by asking the following questions:

1. **Relevance:** What problems are our constituents trying to solve? How does what we do offer a unique or distinctive (partial) solution?

2. **Utilisation:** What is the value chain of our constituents, and how do we amplify results, accelerate speed, or otherwise enhance one or more of the steps in the value chain?

3. **Expertise:** What is our focus area? Where can we prove our benefits?

4. **Ecosystems:** How can we define our product as a platform, which can be configured to solve many types of problems that the user can guide?

Transferring power to your customers or beneficiaries

Open the newspapers of any major Western city, and you're likely to see calls for more teachers, more police, more nurses and more doctors. Who's usually asking? It's most often the public, who want to feel better protected, educated and treated. And, tellingly, it's often the professions themselves, or their unions. But should we listen to them? Are they the best authorities on whether we need more experts?

I'm not for a moment suggesting that police encourage crime to keep themselves in a job, or that doctors and hospitals will try to keep the sick unwell. But health professionals won't always fully use the single most valuable medical tool in their dispensary: The patient. It's a cliché to say that nobody can motivate you except yourself, yet we design, fund and deliver a multitude of services founded on expert-led diagnosis and intervention (not just in health, but in everything from education to financial services). This creates a user-dependence where an admittedly well-meaning provider directs and advises the user, with limited user-independence. Satisfaction increases for a time but, at a certain point, the outcomes of the intervention start to drop off. This is because they're trying to be maintained by the professional, except that they can't be, because they need the user's own motivation and volition to do so. If you doubt me, ask yourself if you've ever had a financial professional prepare a savings or investment plan for you, or a doctor recommend a diet or exercise plan. How well did they do in making you stick to it?

However, there's an irony in all this self-management in today's world. On the one hand, we do far less for ourselves than we used to (think of the number of times you order takeaway or eat out, or the last time you built your own furniture or sewed your own clothing). Mostly, these are products or services that are highly commoditised, meaning they are easily replaceable. On the other hand, we can do a lot *more* for ourselves in a professional sense. For example, I can publish my own books, design my own website, or print my own photos or artwork. In all of these cases, I coordinate and self-manage towards my own self-established goals. What I say to my clients, therefore, is this:

- If your clients need commoditised services that are cheap and convenient (for them, not you), do it for them (or find someone else to).
- If their outcome is a self-established goal, and the support they need is expensive or inconvenient, find new ways of transferring maximum expertise to them.

In this section, we'll focus on the second scenario.

People with chronic health conditions (like heart disease, arthritis or asthma) often have a lower quality of life. These conditions affect mobility and cause pain, impact one's social and economic life, and can even be fatal. In the following diagram, you can see how, if these people simply do nothing (bubble number one in the bottom left-hand corner), the cost is very low, but so are the outcomes. Another approach is to do nothing, and use emergency departments as treatment. Here, effectiveness is good temporarily, but the cost is very high (bubble number two). That leaves two remaining bubbles. First, conventional routine care (bubble number three), in the hands of the health professional. This will definitely yield good, and ongoing, results. However, the cost still remains moderately high. What we are looking for is something that will reduce cost further and turn good results into excellent ones.

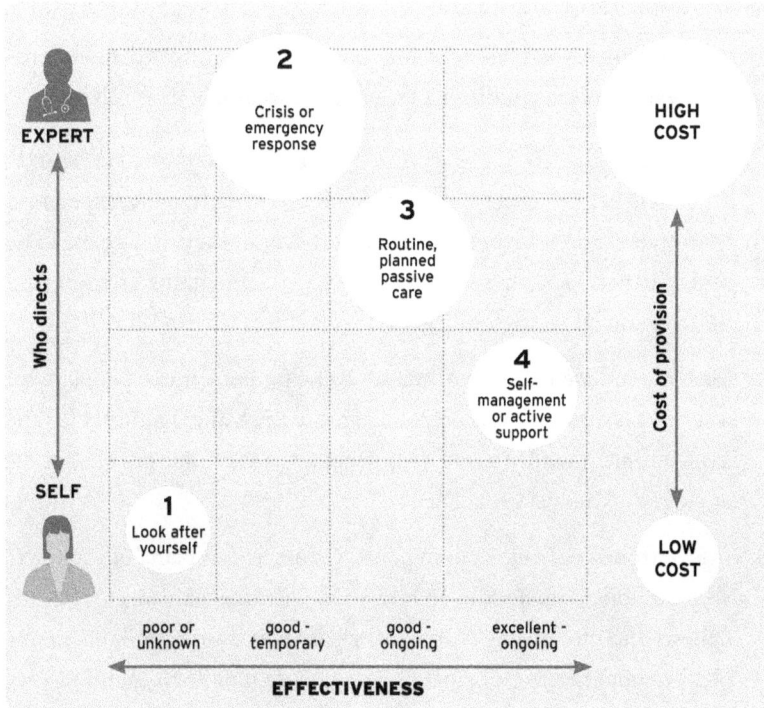

That magic bullet is often increased self-management (bubble number four), whereby people are actively involved in their own healthcare, such as we saw with MOST. For people with chronic conditions who self-manage, we know two things. First, they get better outcomes. That is, they learn how to deal with pain and frustration themselves; they can self-improve their strength, flexibility and endurance; they learn how to use and regulate their medications; they can communicate with family and professionals about their condition; they know what to eat (and what not to); and they know how to evaluate new treatments proposed by their doctors. Second, about eighty per cent of the self-management skills listed above are the same, whether you've got heart disease, diabetes, arthritis or even schizophrenia.

In my experience, there are four practical design features that help providers create the best conditions for people to regulate themselves:

1. The best guides are those who've been there. Programs led by professionals get no better outcomes (and are usually more expensive) than those taught by peer instructors. Second, they don't have to be real. Virtual social networking shows the same gains as in-person networking on some conditions. This is the case with MOST.

2. Sharply reduce mixed messages. Over fifty per cent of people with a serious chronic condition receive more than one diagnosis for the same problem within a one-year period. Create single portals for diagnosis and delivery of advice.

3. Move from knowing to doing, fast. Create action plans or contracts with durability and follow-up measures. Offer mechanisms for self-diagnosis and monitoring with clear trigger points for action (for example, personal health informatics like glucose monitors). Build in successive approximations, feedback, and process improvement supports.

4. It's not enough to work with the person – work with their contexts. The best success in self-management comes from being around exemplars of success (for example, it's hard for overweight people to lose weight when their friends are obese, or for prisoners to go straight while in jail). Surround them with messages that reinforce their actions. Make sure community goals are linked to goals of a health or social service system, with connections to prevention or lifestyle modification.

To maintain and increase levels of self-management among customers or beneficiaries, remember that it's not about managing a specific condition – it's about managing the effects of the conditions that go along with it (like depression and emotional distress). The greatest value in self-management, therefore, is constructively managing the emotional response to the condition, so one of the most powerful things you can do is to build systems that provide assistance in mindfulness and emotional-state management. Such systems could include online forums, but also a combination of peer networks where people are assigned or select 'accountability partners' or 'buddies', formal learning either online (webinars) or physically (workshops) where people learn skills in a social environment, and 'call a friend' methods where people can reach out (via text message, for example) and get a rapid response when they are struggling.

Frequently asked questions

There are two questions I'm often asked about self-management:

1. **But what about clients who really don't know enough to self-manage?**

   This question is about power. I'm often asked, 'But won't experts, practitioners and professionals feel disempowered as they transfer power to their clients, patients and service-users?' Yes, they will, if they continue to see themselves as guardians of secret knowledge or wavers of magic wands.

Another question I'm often asked is: 'Won't they (experts, practitioners and professionals) be rightfully cautious that self-managing patients will absorb a bunch of half-factual urban myths and convince themselves that they're truly the peer of the specialist?' Yes, that also can happen. However, if professionals slowly change their conception of what the ideal role of an expert is, neither of those things will happen. That new role is to see ourselves as builders of systems that hand over primary personal responsibility to our users or clients. If anything, within such a mind shift, the expert has a more important job than ever:

- **Diagnosis:** Reducing the noise and ambiguity of conflicting signals that tell the patient what's really happening.

- **Evidence accumulation:** Establishing best or alternative courses of action.

- **Message creation:** Translating complex and ambivalent material into actionable forms.

- **Navigation:** Holding the hand of a person who's confused by the system and unsure of their optimal path.

- **Resource targeting:** Helping a person access the resources they need.

- **Coordination:** Getting the pieces on the board lined up in a way that makes sense – and gets good results.

2. **We're not a health service, so can our clients still self-manage?**

In another context (like disability, aged care, homelessness, or even problem gambling or crime prevention), self-management will look very different, but the same basic principle applies. That is, behavioural change is not dependent on a condition and its manifestations (pain, poverty level, and so on). Rather, it is dependent on a person's feelings of self-efficacy (a belief that one is capable of performing in a certain way to reach a set of goals).

The power of this is that self-efficacy reinforces itself. For example, 'I believe more in my ability to control my symptoms as I notice my symptoms being controlled.' Even in more transactional public value services (like rubbish collection and library services), the concept of 'Uberisation' is important. This term comes from the well-known ride-sharing service, and refers to any economic or service system where there is an exchange of underutilised capacity of existing assets or human resources (typically through a website or software platform), while incurring only low transaction costs. In the context of rubbish collection, this means that residents could self-manage the quantity and types of rubbish they generate, and the cost and timing of collection.

ACTION TO TAKE

Think about the ways that you can exert leverage in the system in which you operate, focusing on the four key principles outlined earlier:

- Relevance

- Utilisation

- Expertise

- Ecosystems

If you engage directly with users, customers, clients, patients or beneficiaries, there are four key questions to consider:

- How can your service offering remain viable unless you increase the ability of your clients or patients to self-manage?

- How are you actively encouraging self-management among your users?

- How do your professionals balance their roles as experts, as intermediaries and as capacity builders?

- Can you create systems that increase the generic self-management skills of your patients or clients?

CHAPTER 11:

Maximise your impact through partnerships

ANDREW'S OBSERVATION: Many public value organisations adopt a passive approach to partnerships. They consider invitations to partner, but less often do assertive partnering, whereby they initiate the contact, the outcomes and the terms. Then, they notice that they have no influence over their partners. Or they have too many partners. As a result, some public value partnerships don't go deep enough. They remain at a superficial level and don't get strong commitment from their so-called partners. At other times, such partnerships go too far. And at other times still, public value organisations prize their sovereignty when, in fact, it would serve them best to permanently join forces with another organisation. In other words, merge.

The best partnerships are formed out of common cause, for common customers. To quote Lou Gerstner, former CEO of IBM, 'In the end, any organisation is nothing more than the collective capacity of its people to create value.' In his time as CEO, IBM changed strategy so that its pivot point became partnerships, with thirty per cent of its $86 billion in revenue coming from alliances. IBM changed its strategies to embrace alliances, because it saw them as the best way to offer its customers the most valuable and appropriate solutions to their needs – not just the IBM-created option. For instance, IBM has formed alliances with database developers so they can jointly develop, market and sell integrated e-business solutions. But equally, those developers can sell IBM hardware to their customers.

For public value companies, the 'common customer, common cause' approach looks very different. For a start, public sector partnerships are mostly trying to solve what are known as wicked problems (a problem that is difficult or impossible to solve because of incomplete, contradictory and changing requirements, which are often difficult to recognise). What is needed by partners trying to solve youth crime, or run-away mental health issues, or environmental degradation, is both changed thinking and changed action, and these are not to be found within any single organisation. Sometimes, achieving this changed thinking and action is enormously difficult. In my consulting work, I've seen many situations where partners:

- Are not always well intentioned towards each other,
- Aren't always skilled at (or temperamentally inclined towards) agreement,
- Get dragged 'back inside the square' of conventional thought,
- Don't always have similar intellectual capacity, or equal knowledge, about an issue, and
- Aren't always coming from a similar values base.

So, in this chapter, I'll show you how to recruit the right partners so that you can successfully work towards a common cause. You'll also learn how to agree on shared principles, and how to determine the depths of your partnerships.

Common customers, common cause

To work towards a common cause, the most successful public value partnerships are where one organisation takes the lead and assertively enlists the support of various partners. They work together to set the principles of the partnership, and establish rules of reciprocation (what's in it for me?) and adjacency (what else could we offer?). This is largely a textbook fantasy, though, as there are many reasons why it doesn't work nearly so neatly in the real world.

When it comes to forming partnerships, if you're starting from scratch, you would use a more tentative approach (more on this later). If you're already working in a complex operating environment with numerous legacy partners (some of which you might be legislated to work with!), you need to carefully consider how to allocate importance to those partnerships, and even discard existing partnerships if they no longer serve your organisation and its beneficiaries.

I was recently assisting a directorate within a state government health department. Their most senior executive (let's call her Sharon) said, 'Andrew, I'm out of my depth when I don't have authority over my colleagues at my level in parallel agencies.' It turned out Sharon and her team were trying to have 'authority' in all sorts of areas. These included the planning (and funding) of basic health services like hospitals, protecting the population from food- and blood-borne viruses, promoting research, making sure that well-trained health professionals are available, and even getting involved in preventing the long-term determinants of ill health like joblessness and poor housing.

I asked Sharon's team to construct a Partnership Reset Map. This would serve as a visual of their partnerships, with their department at the centre. It had to include:

- **Segments:** A colour-coded segment for each sector they partner with. In their case, there were nine.

- **Layers:** Three concentric layers corresponding to shared influence. The inner ring is where you'll place those partners with whom you share resources and objectives. The middle layer is for those with whom you jointly plan and share capacity-building activities. The outer ring is where you place agencies with whom you share an ecosystem, exchanging information and remaining aware of each other's activities.

- **Dots:** These signify importance. A large dot indicates they are very important to achieve your objectives, while a small dot indicates they're not particularly important.

Sharon placed almost 100 dots on the page, and I've reproduced the diagram here.

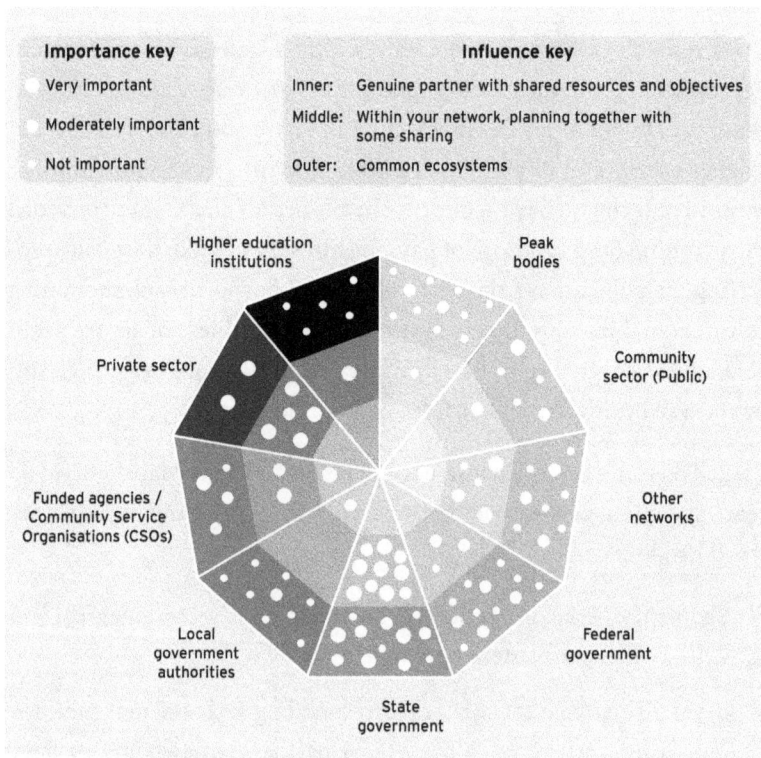

FROM IMPOSSIBLE TO POSSIBLE

This map proved to be diagnostically valuable to the department for two reasons:

1. **Investment of effort:** Sharon could see immediately that her department had a disproportionate level of partnership investment in two areas (the inner circle with medium or large dots and the middle circle with large dots). In the example here, this is a total of eighteen entities.

2. **Identify strategic partnering risks:** The more large dots you have in the outermost ring, the weaker your position is in that area. In other words, having an organisation that is very important for meeting your strategic objectives, but with whom you have low levels of influence, is a considerable strategic risk. Sharon's group had seven entities in the outermost ring.

Note: The dots don't have to represent individual agencies. You are better off thinking of them as types of stakeholders. For example, a single private sector dot might be general practitioners, or a single local government dot might by statutory planners, rather than an individual local government. This also means that you limit the number of dots on your overall map. Having said that, you can then do a separate map (should you wish), focusing on, say, statutory planners, encompassing the twenty local government areas with which you interact (if the statutory planner dot is large enough). You would do this if you felt that one dot didn't capture the variability among the various partners. For instance if you had *some* statutory planners who were very important, some less so, and some in the inner circle, with others on the outer.

The Partnership Reset Map helped the department decide that it didn't really have any role in four of the existing partnerships (small dots in the middle ring) but, most importantly, that it should redefine and rebuild its role in relation to the seven large dots in the outer ring. Sharon had previously said she didn't have influence, but now felt like she had a clear roadmap to build from. A year in, she had succeeded in gaining significant trust from five of the seven outer ring partners by engaging with them in two ways: Articulating why they're important, and bringing them into the middle ring by focusing on shared objectives and resources.

There are many instances where, fortunately, you don't need to reset partnerships because they've weakened through neglect, but simply start building them. It is helpful to think of three types of partners: Delivery partners, supportive partners and adjacent partners. Girls Who Code (a non-profit organisation which aims to support and increase the number of women in computer science) has built delivery partnerships with AT&T, Microsoft, Facebook and sixty other firms. These are desirable partners, because they offer *different* things that provide *complementary value* directly to the beneficiary (in this case, each individual girl or woman). GWC provides the educational and motivational framework, while the companies provide a realistic employment context, physical sites and mentors. In doing so, each offering amplifies the value of the other. The end results are then *reciprocal*. The likes of Facebook and Microsoft build a pipeline of employable women, and GWC moves a few dozen women closer to its goal of one million women entering STEM (science, technology, engineering and mathematics) professions.

So, if you're planning to work with delivery partners, check for:

- **Reciprocal results:** Are they different, but aligned, and highly relevant to the customer or user?
- **Different capabilities:** Are each of you providing what the other *doesn't* offer?
- **Complementary value:** Does the capability you provide magnify theirs, and vice versa?

Delivery partners are easy to conceive because they, like you, work directly with your customers, fulfilling aspects of the value chain that *you do not*. *Supportive* partners are those who provide a means to your ends, usually not because you don't provide these services, but because you simply *can't*. These are the sorts of partners with specialist expertise that you lack, possibly because it's simply not worth specialising in that area. For instance, research, capital raising, technology, or consulting advice on specific topics like marketing and brand presence, business development or people development.

The third category of partner consists of what I call *adjacent* partners. These are relationships formed with entities that provide what the core business *chooses not to provide*. For example, Dress for Success is very confident in its focus, and recognises that many of its beneficiaries require access to homeless shelters, domestic violence shelters, universities and other educational institutions, and job training programs. The organisation consequently sets up referral, recommendation and preferred supplier relationships with such organisations, on a local basis and organised by each affiliate, but to a consistent method of 'common client, common cause'.

When you want to build up the most appropriate partnerships, whether they are delivery, supportive or adjacent partnerships, the same basic process applies. The 'dealmaker' mindset will tempt many to begin in the wrong place by getting straight into discussing activities and terms. The conversation will go like this: 'What if we were to do X, and you were to do Y? That way, you'd get A, and we'd get B. Wouldn't that be great?'

In my experience, once the basic area of partnership is agreed to be worthwhile, it is far better to begin with a discussion of principles. These are not airy-fairy motherhood statements featuring words like 'respect' and 'transparency'. Rather, they become the terms of engagement that describe how the partners will approach the many complexities of partnering well.

Agreeing on principles

Facebook founder Mark Zuckerberg has told of how he and his now COO, Sheryl Sandberg, met for long, weekly after-dinner conversations for months before they decided to work together. What did they discuss? Very little content, mostly process. They agreed on how they would establish priorities, set direction and focus, resolve disagreements, and present cases for new initiatives, understanding that the content of the company's direction, focus and initiatives (and disagreements) was utterly unpredictable at the time of their discussions. All they knew is that they would have all sorts of content they'd have to successfully partner on.

Agreeing on principles is a way for more formal partnerships to form between organisations. Let me give you another example. A public hospital client wanted to partner on a variety of services, like oncology treatment, with a smaller, regional hospital. The reciprocal benefit was that the smaller community would have access to best-of-breed treatment locally, and the larger hospital would have less demand from people within that region, thereby shortening its wait times. They determined that twelve partnership principles would guide their work over the coming three years, as they set up and operated this joint oncology service:

1. Put client and community at the centre. Demonstrably improve the client **experience** or **outcome**.

2. **Empower.** If staff see opportunity, they may take initiative, increasing capability or development of staff (separately and jointly).

3. **Optimise.** Measurably heighten quality, efficiency or effectiveness.

4. Create **financial sustainability** and mutual economic benefit. This includes creating new market opportunities.

5. Promote **excellence.** Instil confidence that each organisation can bring clinical excellence.

6. Enable **collaboration.** We are non-exclusive collaborators, and, when competing (or not collaborating), do so transparently.

7. Preserve **independence.** We retain separate identities as the situation demands and respect for each other's aspirations.

8. Agree on **risk.** Create and adhere to structured ways of monitoring or resolving risk.

9. Maintain **equality** and **transparency.** Uphold mutual respect and equality of power (including agreed ways of behaving).

10. Remain **ethical** and legal. All transactions must comply with requirements.

11. Achieve **longevity.** Maintain organisational continuity across multiple projects, ensuring partnerships survive turnover of staff or boards.

12. **Communicate** with stakeholders effectively. Release information at the same time, and publicly announce alliances within their scope.

These partnership principles are deliberately non-legalistic, so that they do not replace a memorandum of understanding or legal contract. The purpose here is to establish behavioural expectations among executives and senior clinicians. From this foundation, six further agreements can be reached:

- Common objectives
- Metrics
- Resourcing
- Workforce
- Change
- Next steps

Here is a sample agreement for the oncology partnership. The way that the group reached agreement was to bring together interested parties from several levels: At least one director-level sponsor, the responsible executives, relevant managers, and several content specialists (in this case, clinicians).

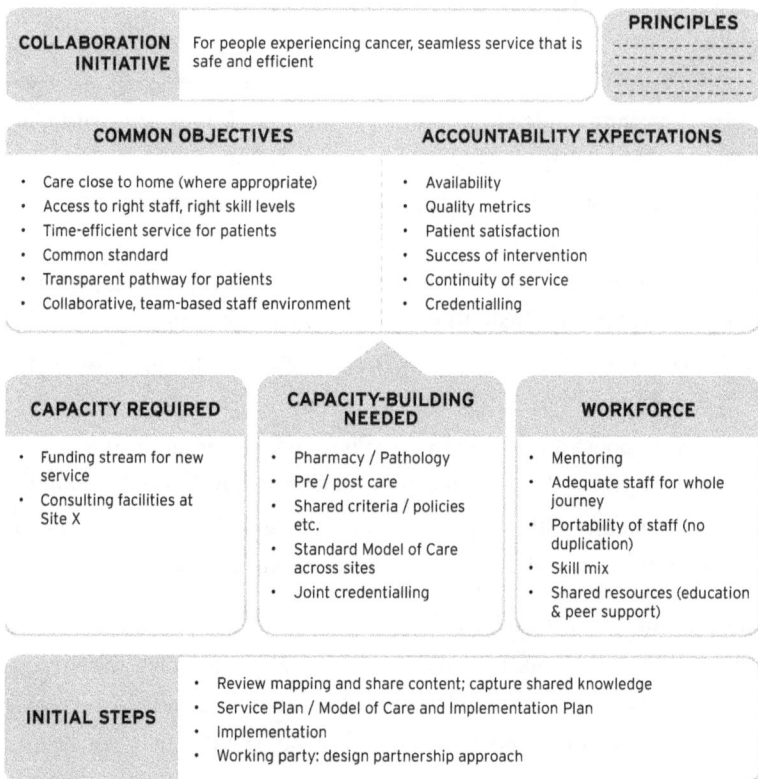

COLLABORATION INITIATIVE	For people experiencing cancer, seamless service that is safe and efficient	PRINCIPLES

COMMON OBJECTIVES	ACCOUNTABILITY EXPECTATIONS
• Care close to home (where appropriate) • Access to right staff, right skill levels • Time-efficient service for patients • Common standard • Transparent pathway for patients • Collaborative, team-based staff environment	• Availability • Quality metrics • Patient satisfaction • Success of intervention • Continuity of service • Credentialling

CAPACITY REQUIRED	CAPACITY-BUILDING NEEDED	WORKFORCE
• Funding stream for new service • Consulting facilities at Site X	• Pharmacy / Pathology • Pre / post care • Shared criteria / policies etc. • Standard Model of Care across sites • Joint credentialling	• Mentoring • Adequate staff for whole journey • Portability of staff (no duplication) • Skill mix • Shared resources (education & peer support)

INITIAL STEPS	• Review mapping and share content; capture shared knowledge • Service Plan / Model of Care and Implementation Plan • Implementation • Working party: design partnership approach

In addition to determining the *focus* of the various partnerships you enter, it's also important to determine the *depth* of these partnerships. In the next section, we'll look at the latter, as this is a common conundrum for public value organisations.

Determining the depths of your partnerships

UNICEF engages in a broad range of partnerships and collaborative relationships, including global program partnerships, which have a tremendously wide reach. It links up governmental and non-governmental organisations, community-based organisations, civic movements and advocacy groups, trade unions, faith-based organisations and professional voluntary associations, the corporate sector, and other entities such as the media and knowledge institutions. The essential starting point, as always, is focus. UNICEF has five key focus areas:

1. Young child survival and development.
2. Basic education and gender equality.
3. Reducing HIV/AIDS among children.
4. Child protection from violence, exploitation and abuse.
5. Policy advocacy and partnerships for children's rights.

Against each of these are more detailed areas of focus, based on UNICEF's value chain. For instance, in the value chain for child survival and development, there are nutrition partnerships, clean water partnerships, health partnerships and emergency response partnerships. UNICEF answers the question of what to commit to by considering the following levels of partnership:

- **Project cooperation:** Where partners possess local, on-the-ground delivery capability that is not easily replaceable.
- **Extending reach and effectiveness:** Where a wicked problem is simply insurmountable, partners can build on adjacent roles.
- **Technology knowledge and innovative practice:** Where new ways have to be found to make an impact.

- **Advocating and engaging in policy dialogue:** Where mobilising political will at the national level, and promoting social and behavioural change at the community level, is required.
- **Child participation and engagement:** Where children need to participate in decision making that affects them, and to have their voices heard by decision makers at the highest levels.
- **Civil society development:** Where entire local systems require stimulating to achieve desired results.
- **Small-scale support:** Where small and informal partnership groups achieve on-the-ground quick wins using grants below $10,000, with a low administrative burden.
- **Private sector resource mobilisation:** Where cash from corporate supporters is applied to specific UNICEF campaigns.

You may not be a global, multibillion-dollar organisation with a vision to eradicate an entire class of wicked problems, but the same principles apply in terms of how to think about *depths of partnership*.

In a recent confidential discussion, a client (a CEO named Monica) asked me, 'What would your opinion be of us and Agency X merging?'

This was the first time I had heard of this as a possibility, despite having worked with this organisation's board and executive team for some months. So, I simply asked, 'Why?'

Monica paused before responding, 'Well, they approached us. We weren't expecting it. But we have similar clients, although in different geographies. And we could achieve some backend efficiency, I think.'

I wanted to say, 'You're thinking of committing to marriage before you've been on a date!'

What I said instead was, 'That's a good start, Monica. You've named two reasons why you may want an alliance with Agency X. Would it be helpful if I showed you twenty typical reasons why organisations ally, and then you can form a view about the most appropriate level of partnership commitment you might want?'

She agreed that would be helpful, and so I showed her a diagram like this one, saying, 'You don't want to go too far too soon. Nor do you want to not go far enough with Agency X. Let's work through this from bottom to top.'

How strong an alliance is best?

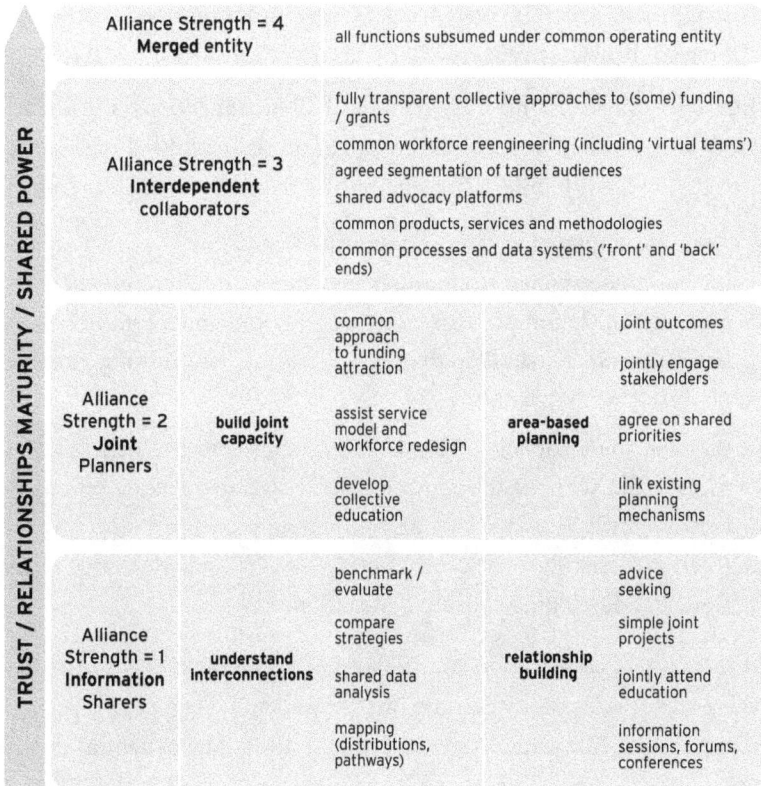

TRUST / RELATIONSHIPS MATURITY / SHARED POWER

Alliance Strength = 4 **Merged** entity	all functions subsumed under common operating entity			
Alliance Strength = 3 **Interdependent collaborators**	fully transparent collective approaches to (some) funding / grants common workforce reengineering (including 'virtual teams') agreed segmentation of target audiences shared advocacy platforms common products, services and methodologies common processes and data systems ('front' and 'back' ends)			
Alliance Strength = 2 **Joint Planners**	**build joint capacity**	common approach to funding attraction assist service model and workforce redesign develop collective education	**area-based planning**	joint outcomes jointly engage stakeholders agree on shared priorities link existing planning mechanisms
Alliance Strength = 1 **Information Sharers**	**understand interconnections**	benchmark / evaluate compare strategies shared data analysis mapping (distributions, pathways)	**relationship building**	advice seeking simple joint projects jointly attend education information sessions, forums, conferences

I explained to Monica that I use the term 'alliance strength' to suggest different levels of partnership commitment. The lowest level is information sharing, with low levels of commitment. In this instance, value arises from:

- **Relationship building.** This creates trust and a sense of common purpose at varying levels, and can be achieved in many ways – advice seeking, simple joint projects, jointly attended education, and information sessions, forums and conferences.

- **Understanding interconnections.** This leverages information or intelligence held by one organisation for the benefit of the other, and can include benchmarking and evaluation, comparing strategies, shared data analysis, evidence gathering and translation, and mapping of clients or needs.

Only once the relationship is built, and interconnections are understood, is it perhaps worthwhile investigating the next level of alliance strength, which is jointly planning. In this instance, value arises from:

- **Area-based planning.** This enables the 'joined forces' of two organisations to be applied to common customers, and therefore includes agreeing on shared priorities, setting joint outcomes, jointly engaging stakeholders, shared advocacy platforms, and linking existing planning mechanisms.

- **Building joint capacity.** This is getting closer to the benefits of a merger, but without the commitment to dissolve at least one partner's identity. This can include common approaches to funding attraction, assisting each other's service model and workforce redesign, and developing collective education.

At this level of cooperation, a third level of partnership may eventuate, where the organisations become interdependent collaborators, acting, in some ways, like a single 'virtual' organisation. The benefit of this is that every gain from a collective approach is maximised, so that incoming and outgoing resources are best utilised with minimal duplication. This may involve:

- Fully transparent collective approaches to (some) funding or grants.
- Common workforce reengineering (including virtual teams).
- Agreed segmentation of target audiences.
- Common products, services and methodologies.
- Common processes and data systems (frontend and backend).

Organisational partnerships are a lot like relationships. Don't move in with someone (become an interdependent collaborator) when, in fact, you're not at all convinced that information sharing will work for you both. Ascend the levels carefully and prudently – not necessarily slowly, but with conscious thought and deliberation.

You may discover that a one-dimensional alliance will not serve your purposes. In other words, you might wish to use the alliance strength table as a menu, and create a combination of information sharing, some joint planning, and just one or two aspects of interdependent collaboration.

You may have noticed a fourth level in the alliance strength table: Merged entity. For a refresher on the pros and cons of mergers, I encourage you to re-read the section in Chapter 3 titled 'To merge or not to merge?'.

Frequently asked questions

There are four common questions I receive about partnerships:

1. **Can you have a partnership without strong trust?**

    No. To collaborate on wicked problems requires substantial trust and mutual commitment among the parties. Trust increases the probability that parties will feel comfortable about revealing information that may make them vulnerable to opportunistic behaviour by other parties. To the extent that they trust each other, actors will be more likely to take the risk of disclosing such information, thereby enhancing the extent to which differential knowledge is brought to bear on the problem.

2. **What if my partners don't fulfil their part?**

If this happens, it's a sign that you haven't made a compelling case for the partnership. Specifically, you haven't identified the complementary benefit for the beneficiary, or you haven't worked out the reciprocal benefits for each partner. Frequently, too, this is a sign that you neglected to set principles, or that the principles you set are missing some important elements. In such a case, it's vital to bring your concerns to the attention of the other party. Ask them about the perceived value, because it may be that their focus has shifted, so that what was important to them initially is less so, or that the person who initially spearheaded their commitment has moved on.

What is most important is that you agree, ahead of time, on what process you will follow when one party has a grievance against the other. Typically, this will involve an escalating set of solutions, from raising awareness, to joint problem solving, to sanctions or limits placed on one of the partners and, if a resolution can't be reached, ultimately dissolution of the partnership. I strongly believe that organisations are better off following a staged process than simply being avoidant and letting the partnership fall into disrepair.

3. **What if a partnership is obligatory, but we're not seeing the value?**

This is the most common issue I see in obligatory partnerships. Governments will establish a partnership framework and will authorise small amounts of investment to attract partners. Such partnerships then accumulate. In the most extreme instance of this I've encountered, a state government, over ten years, authorised successive layers of partnerships designed to support children and families who are vulnerable and disadvantaged. Each partnership has a slightly different emphasis, similar membership, but the same target audience. By the time I was working with them, the number of partnerships had grown to forty-eight. Thirty-three people were employed full-time to coordinate these partnerships, and partners spent 5,000 hours a year in over 250 meetings. The forty-eight partnerships eventually became just four. If you're not able to achieve such significant streamlining, at least you can do what Sharon did. Assess the value of each partnership, and increase or decrease your commitment accordingly.

4. **How important is cultural compatibility in partnerships?**

It's almost the most important factor, especially in public value partnerships. The most important aspects of bringing two cultures together is finding common cause, honestly discussing differences, and predicting required changes. Each of these requires a strong process.

We've already discussed how to find a common cause, so I won't repeat that information here. Honestly discussing differences works best from both a 'self' and 'other' perspective. How I've done that in the past is by asking Agency A to sum up what makes them unique or distinctive, and also to sum up what makes Agency B unique or distinctive. I encourage them to speak honestly, warts and all! Agency B will do it for Agency A as well; in the same room, at the same time. This breaks down myths that each agency holds about the other tremendously well, and prevents a huge number of potential conflicts.

In one case, I heard cash-strapped Agency A tell Agency B that they saw Agency B as well resourced, and therefore able to weather ups and downs in revenue very easily. The executives from Agency B looked at each other knowingly before responding, 'We almost became insolvent last year. We were down to two months of cash.' This created a strong sense of being in the same boat, and reoriented some of the partnership objectives towards greater efficiency and cost-savings.

The third discussion is equally vital: If we do X together, what may (or will) require change for us (or them) is _____. At best, this will build commonality across teams. At worst, it will highlight where bridges need to be built, or where rivers simply can't be crossed right now. In a recent example, one partner said to the other, 'If we change our workforce configurations this year, it will require you to raise salaries to maintain parity with us.' This led to a serious conversation about how best to resolve this, and it was agreed that both partners would merge their workforces for that service area under a single umbrella. So, in essence, a partial merger.

ACTION TO TAKE

Partnerships are a vital aspect of governmental, non-profit and other public value work, as you are invariably solving wicked problems. Consequently, you should check that you've done the following internal and external thinking.

PLANNING YOUR PARTNERSHIPS (INTERNAL THINKING)

1. Ask yourself whether you can best achieve your purpose alone, or with others. Be honest and realistic, by answering the following questions:

- What **won't** we do? (These are the limits to your purpose.)

- What **don't** we do? (These are limits to your role, scope or scale.)

- What **can't** we do? (These are limits to your capabilities or capacity.)

- Who does/will/could?

2. Map your partners, both existing and potential. The value of a simple visual display can't be underestimated in getting people to work together. Here are some points to consider:

   - What levels of partnership are going to serve you best? Make a list and court appropriate partners. It may be helpful to quantify the resource you are committing to various partnerships by simply counting hours, personnel, in-kind support, and dollar contributions you make.

   - If you're weak (lacking in strong balance sheets, cashflows, service contracts, management systems, intellectual property or goodwill), look for an acquirer. Quantify your value in each of these categories.

   - If you're strong, do at least a cursory scan of potential takeover targets. List them. Approach them. Do the paper or whiteboard exercise on how to consider merging, outlined in Chapter 3.

IMPROVING YOUR PARTNERSHIPS (EXTERNAL THINKING)

3. Check that you've got the right principles. If you've never articulated these, it's not too late to do so. You can build this process into a review or 'health check' of the partnership.

4. Reset your partnerships by consciously improving on those that are important, and reducing your commitment to those that are less significant.

CHAPTER 12:

Shamelessly build your profile

ANDREW'S OBSERVATION: Compared to the most visible brands (think Apple, Tesla or IKEA), public value organisations feel invisible, unknown or even maligned. This is because many are not confident about what they're outstanding at. Even if they are, they don't systematically turn their outstanding results into evidence. They are rarely clear on what associations they want their brand to have nor do they maximise competitiveness, either because they don't have a great story or don't know how to tell it.

Many years ago, I was told by someone far older and wiser than me: 'Bureaucrats seek evidence; politicians want stories.' This distinction has never been lost on me, and, while useful, it's obvious that all successful public value organisations use *both* to best advantage. That's the focus of this chapter.

Painting a vivid picture through numbers

Unless you're an accountant, or in business development, you probably don't find spreadsheets compelling, and many leaders in mission-driven organisations do not see themselves as 'numbers people'. But numbers, used judiciously, can paint a vibrant picture of your mission – and your achievements.

The Acumen venture capital fund has the purpose of solving poverty, sustainably. It's a big claim, and with 'only' $100 million to invest[14], it needs to provide critical before-and-after evidence that its investments

---

14 It sounds like a lot of money, but to put it into perspective, the Bill & Melinda Gates Foundation, which also tackles global poverty, invests $4.5 billion *in a single year.*

create the desired impact. Acumen thrives on evidence creation, with a separate arm of its organisation focused solely on impact measurement. It subscribes to big-picture measures of success such as the Progress out of Poverty Index, which provides evidence that its overall purpose is met, but it also measures the success at an individual investment level.

One of its investments aims to fill dark Ugandan villages with light. Just five per cent of rural Ugandans are connected to a national power grid, which frequently suffers brownouts and blackouts. Those not connected have to make do with expensive and often dangerous alternatives such as kerosene. To solve this problem, Acumen invested in a micro-financed solar business called SolarNow. Once up and running, Acumen asked the question: How do we know this works?

It focused on three data points that help build the profile of SolarNow:

- Are the *poorest people* accessing this? Yes. Half of SolarNow's 8,000 customers are living on less than $2.50 per person per day, indicating a strong reach into even the poorest rural communities.

- Are they getting *more light*? Yes. All customers reported an increase in hours of available lighting, with the average customer experiencing an increase of two hours of light per day.

- Are they *replacing* dirtier, more dangerous and more expensive light sources? Yes. On average, customers move from six hours of light from non-SolarNow sources, to only one hour per day.

A powerful story has been built by SolarNow from these three data points, which essentially says: Even if you are among the poorest of families, you can afford to light your house all evening. What is important here is that the numbers capture the essence of SolarNow's theory of change. Similarly, to tell a profile-building story through data, you need to show that your interventions lead to the result sought, and that this is in keeping with your organisation's fundamental purpose. Doing so will not only keep you and your people focused, but it helps immeasurably with gaining support, both political and financial. Quantitative information is an essential and powerful profile-builder, because it shows you're making progress. But the data alone has limited effect. It needs to be used to construct a powerful story. Let me give you another example, focusing specifically on the storytelling element.

New Story is an organisation that funds and builds $6,000 houses for slum dwellers in Latin America. Its theory of change recognises that housing is a social determinant of myriad other successes for a family, including education attainment, wellbeing, income and community connection. So, New Story measures each of these in its impact data. Its theory of change also recognises that families will be more stable when a house allows them water, sanitation, electricity and healthcare. So, yes, this is measured too, before and after. The family's income is also examined based on the occupational breakdown and monthly household income. The impact data also assesses children's access to schools, as well as attendance and performance. Community building is also considered. Potential investors are shown the faces and stories of the families who will be receiving the houses, and asked for their input on how the houses should be built. In all, a comprehensive 'data picture' is built up.

This data picture is done for every family. Not just because each house is tailor-made for a specific set of people, but because New Story wants to emphasise the human side by putting a name on each of the houses built. New Story wants you and me, the investors, to know exactly what we are getting for our money. They want us to meet the people who will benefit from the houses, so that we understand and appreciate the long-term impact of our investment. They even provide us with video footage as evidence, to make sure we know how much we have helped, and they reassure us that 100 per cent of the money we donate will go to the construction of the houses, since New Story's operating costs are funded elsewhere.

Both Acumen and New Story highlight the power of translating your numbers into meaningful stories. In other words, turning the information you give to bureaucrats into the stories you tell politicians. But how do you ensure your stories appeal to your desired target market, and stick?

Finding your stickiness

The key to a good story is stickiness. One organisation known for its effective storytelling is Zeal, in Auckland, New Zealand, whose mission is to positively impact young people through creativity. This includes building their own narratives of what it means to be young, the challenges they face, and how to overcome these challenges in order to build a better world.

Zeal's website is full of blogs and videos (documentaries, music videos and commentary) produced by young people themselves. The organisation's suicide prevention work is called Live for Tomorrow, and features a series of very 'sticky' videos called 'The Great Mental Health Experiment'. It's deliberately low-budget and irreverent. Bureaucrats and social services administrators would call it authentic. Zeal is targeting a very specific group of young people, and has almost 1,000 subscribers to this video series alone, with 250,000 views. Zeal's Live for Tomorrow photo challenge attracted 7,800 posts and over three million views. That's a whole lot more than if it had published a series of bland pamphlets, or stuck notices on community centre pin-up boards.

We should bother with stickiness because stories activate our empathic response, and are also memorable. The secrets to stickiness, as a way of building your organisation's profile, are remarkably simple. Yet I notice that many public value organisations don't observe these, or aren't aware that they're needed.

Here are six secrets to 'sticky', effective storytelling:

1. **Feature real people.** The story should describe, or clearly imply, what problem is being solved, why it's a problem, and what you've done to solve the problem and why that failed.

2. **Tell the story in first person.** The highest-impact stories are those told by the people themselves. This could be via an interview, a blog post or a video.

3. **Focus on plain language.** Write the way people speak. Test out the stories on students in years seven and eight. Do they get it? Even if you're aiming to convince policymakers or academics of your credentials, they will welcome ease and simplicity.

4. **Find the hook.** Every story should have a punch or a kick to it. Find something that acts as a focal point for the story. Or, better yet, find a story with a powerful hook that exemplifies your purpose.

5. **Be specific.** Give names. Give numbers. Compare before and after.

6. **Be vivid.** Label feelings. Use provocative language if that's appropriate. Be critical of 'sacred cows' and be willing to bust myths.

Too many public value stories are called 'case studies', and are white-washed and bland approximations of the true human achievement that they're trying to convey. Remember, the stories you tell should clearly show movement from impossible to possible. Here's an example from one of Dress for Success's alumni, Paula Gonzales:

'My mother gave birth to me when she was only fourteen years old. But I never knew her as a mother. You see, my mother was not just my mother.

She was also my sister. At the dawn of her adulthood, she was raped by her father – by my father. I suffered through nine years of severe domestic violence, and faced abuse from my great-grandmother herself, who had raised me. I contemplated suicide many times.

'It seemed as if a cycle had been created with my mother because, at the age of fourteen, I too became pregnant. But then I realised that being a single, teenage mother with a broken background wasn't an excuse as to why I wouldn't be able to succeed in life, it was the reason why I had to.

'When I came to Dress for Success, I made a commitment to more than just myself and even to more than just my family. Whether someone knew me as family, a friend or just a woman they passed on the street, I wanted to be an example of excellence for everyone that never had any-one. As a young mother who had a baby on each hip, people used to call me a "nobody" and tell me that I'd never amount to anything.

'Well, this "nobody" had two high school diplomas, an Associate's de-gree and was the boss of her own business before she turned 30, all while raising five children, now along with the help of my husband, Alejandro. And I'm leading a new generation of business owners. What I am pass-ing down is the power of perseverance. I didn't have any professional role models growing up as a girl, but my daughter does. All of my five children do. That role model is me.'

It's powerful stuff, isn't it? Dress for Success has processes in place to capture such stories, as it understands that these are the lifeblood of its affiliate system. Women simply get together at events and share stories. They're published in annual reports, told to journalists, and relayed in blog posts, podcasts and YouTube videos. Can you do the same by har-vesting the stories of your clients, packaging them, and then sending them out through various channels to your future clients, your partners, and investors or supporters?

One way to work out which stories you want to tell is to think about ownership. What cause do you want to 'own'? Zeal, for example, 'owns' youth creativity in New Zealand. Dress for Success 'owns' empowered women entering the workforce. On a more local level, Sunbury Community Health wants to own 'social fabric' in just a single township of 50,000 people.

Regardless of what you own, there are clear practices that work best in claiming ownership, or, to put it more formally, becoming an issues leader:

1. **Label stuff.** Define it, and name it. This is how ideas-ownership occurs, and it's one way in which IHI is streets ahead of its competitors. It gives everything a name, including its campaigns (such as the 100,000 Lives Campaign).

2. **Be generous.** Give your ideas away freely. Publish research papers. Present at conferences. Convene round tables and think tanks of those you want to work with, and those you want to impress. Produce models and frameworks. Invite others into your tent to see how you do it. In Australia, the Brotherhood of St Laurence has a mandate to 'end poverty', and it has an impressive body of research, presentations and position statements to this end.

3. **Break things.** Not actual things, but ideas. You know what the sacred cows of your sector are. Challenge them. Adopt contrarian thinking and bust myths. The Health Issues Centre, whose role we looked at in Chapter 2, is a good case in point. They are not frightened of standing for something that they know they can verify. If you don't know what 'big ideas' you could stand for, ask your most outspoken frontline people to tell you. In my experience, they won't hold back. If you're

anxious about being a tall poppy and disenfranchising supporters or investors, ensure you do it in a balanced way, and test for external support for your views. Remember that all social good, or public value, is inherently critical of something – you only exist because something in society is broken or suboptimal. So, name it and claim it.

Frequently asked questions

There are four questions that my clients routinely ask me about building their profile, and about being better understood and recognised.

1. **If we're new to this, how should we start to source material for a stickier profile?**

   There are two *wrong* places to start. One is your strategic and business plans. Typically, organisations that populate their websites and other marketing collateral with vision statements and strategic priorities fail to engage anyone. These statements are designed to be *accurate*, not *compelling*. The other wrong place to start is by creating a comprehensive evidence base by building an entire outcomes framework, or fully featured evaluation model. This will slow you down, and you'll get bogged down in only building profile around what you can measure, which isn't the totality of your value. You may also fall for the 'metrics myth', which is a belief in a holy grail of metrics that could tell your story, if only you could articulate them, or measure them.

   Instead, I advise clients to look deeply into their purpose, their theory of change and their desired results areas, and work backwards from that. Even a single point of interest (a data point or a story) can be 'farmed' to yield a wealth of social media posts, publications or talking points.

2. Do we need a strong brand?

Yes, you do. This doesn't mean merely a logo, designated colours and fonts, and a tagline as identifiable as 'Taste the Feeling' (Coca-Cola) or 'Just Do It' (Nike). Nor does it mean spending $40 million on a famous spokesperson like George Clooney, as Nespresso did to promote its upmarket coffee pods. But it does mean that all your touchpoints with stakeholders (customers, but also investors and partners) must reflect the associations you desire with your brand. To get to a deeper understanding of this, I recommend my clients answer five sets of questions:

- What would a strong(er) brand achieve for us in our service area?
- Who are our customers now? What customers do we want to have? Are these different? What problems are we solving for our customers?
- What are the functional benefits we offer? What are the emotional benefits?
- When people think about us, what are the feelings and associations we want them to have? What kind of 'personality' do we want our brand to have?
- What changes to our story would need to happen to achieve more in our sector/s?

You can ask various informants these questions, including staff, customers (both current and potential), supporters, funders and investors. Their answers, once distilled, will guide you in determining four things:

- **Brand architecture:** This is the structure of your various brands and their relationship with each other. One client of mine had sixty-three different brands, most with completely different logos and styles. Needless to say, this was a nightmare to maintain and their visibility suffered, as their clients saw themselves as clients of Service A or B or C, but not of the organisation, which was largely invisible to them.

- **Visual identity:** This is your brand's look and feel – a signature style made up of colour, imagery and typefaces, intended to convey an ethos linked to the emotional benefits, desired feelings and associations.

- **Ambassadors:** These are people you recruit to represent your brand in a positive light, and by doing so help to increase brand awareness and attract support. They possess attributes that are consistent with the associations you desire. They may be paid or unpaid, humble or inspirational, present in person (for example, at events) or merely visually (such as in photos).

- **Storytelling:** The articulation of benefits and key customers will help you determine which stories are likely to gain traction, especially if you can craft them as before-and-after stories.

3. **What's the single most powerful way to build our profile?**

Customer advocacy, hands down. Passionate consumers or beneficiaries are your best advocates, and gaining them is strongly correlated to both customer gain and profitability. You should absolutely find ways to listen to customers' support of you, so that you can use it to enhance your profile.

The Net Promoter Score, developed by Fred Reichheld, is one of the simplest loyalty measures. Customers are asked: How likely is it that you would recommend us to a friend or colleague? They must then provide a rating from zero ('Not at all likely') to ten ('Extremely likely').

The measure is called the 'net promoter' score because detractors are subtracted from promoters. Detractors are defined as respondents who provide a rating of six or lower, with promoters only those who rated a nine or ten. (Respondents who selected seven or eight are considered neutral.) The NPS measure can run from zero per cent (zero per cent promoters, 100 per cent detractors) to 100 per cent (100 per cent promoters, zero per cent detractors), with average measures in the twenty to forty per cent range, with strong variation depending on industry[15]. The companies with the most loyal customers score seventy per cent plus (in the US, Amazon and Apple are both in this elite league, with Costco at the top of the table at nearly eighty per cent).

Some people believe NPS is not relevant to non-profits and government agencies because the repeat purchasing that drives loyalty for commercial businesses is not the desire for public value organisations. That is true. However, research has been done in anti-poverty organisations to show that promoters take three times more steps towards their goals than detractors. Promoters also achieve five times more progress than detractors. While there are many arguments concerning whether to subtract detractors from promoters, the core issue here is that it is absolutely worth measuring levels of support for your organisation. The reality is that when you solve people's problems, completely and remarkably, they will want to talk about it.

4. What holds people back from building profile?

Most people would say money first, skills second, time third. I'd argue it's a bit of all of these, but they all miss the real root cause,

15 Some of the industries with the worst average NPSs are internet providers and telcos (under twenty per cent), and banks and credit cards (under twenty-five per cent).

which is lack of confidence. Public value organisations just aren't that skilled at blowing their own horn. They honestly and rightfully believe they're doing good work, but they don't take the time to think deeply about how to describe their purpose, their role, their theory of change, their result areas, and the evidence and stories that demonstrate they're getting great results. As a consequence, they complain about being a 'best kept secret'. To build confidence, I advise my clients to do three things:

- **Connect to the work.** Every month, or every quarter, build a formalised process that gives senior people deep insight into problems solved. Those people are often far removed from the coalface and are not at all aware of gritty realities, nor the profound benefits that simple outcomes represent for people. The process may include site visits, presentations from former or current clients, benchmarking studies or video testimonials.

- **Publish something – anything at all to start with.** Share facts and figures. Bust some myths. Tell stories. Interview your clients, or your best workers, or your new hires, or your best donors, or your most experienced volunteers. Get this material into the hands of ten people, then 100, then 1,000. Use blogs, email newsletters, podcasts, slides and videos. You could even take the radical step of using paper. Make publication and dissemination of ideas every business unit's work, not just the work of a strategic communications team. Eventually, you can package your products together into manifestos, frameworks, or 'bibles'.

- **Ask why.** In team meetings, executive briefings and strategic update sessions, bring the focus back to the people who are your beneficiaries. When you talk about reducing waitlist times, make it more than a quantitative discussion. Talk about the human impact of keeping someone waiting weeks for a physiotherapy appointment. Then, when you've reduced wait times by a week, use these as stories you can publicise.

ACTION TO TAKE

An entire book could be written on profile-building for public value organisations. However, I strongly believe that if you answer the following five questions brutally honestly with your staff, you will be streets ahead of other competing organisations:

1. Are you susceptible to the metrics myth (the belief that 'If only we had the right metrics, we'd be able to tell our story')? Instead, can you identify a handful of data points around which to tell a powerful story?

2. What non-quantitative stories can you tell? How can you make them sticky?

3. What are the desired associations with your brand? How effectively does your brand currently achieve this?

4. What issue do you 'own' or lead on? What intellectual property are you making freely available?

5. How can you enlist your customers as supporters?

CHAPTER 13:

Creating a meritocracy of ideas

ANDREW'S OBSERVATION: Many organisations end up promoting poor ideas because they don't know what a good idea looks like, or because they're not comparing it to enough alternatives. Even when they have good ideas, they don't have consistent ways to win the hearts and minds of their customers or beneficiaries and have these ideas adopted en masse. Consequently, their ideas stall or, worse, are resisted. To stop this from happening, you need to create a meritocracy of ideas. To explain what I mean by that, allow me to share a story with you.

I love foreign supermarkets. In Paris recently, with my niece, Ava, we were shopping for some supper ingredients late at night, both of us jet-lagged. We had just trawled past the extraordinary cheese cabinet when suddenly Ava stopped dead in her tracks.

'Oh my god!' she muttered under her breath. 'I can't believe it!'

I looked to see what exotic delicacy had grabbed her attention.

'Yes, yes, yes! This is the best, best, best thing ever, Uncle Andrew.'

She held up a small plastic bottle with a familiar logo on it. It was a Starbucks Frappuccino.

'You can't buy these in Australia,' she went on breathlessly. 'My friends won't believe it.'

As she picked off a few different flavours, I marvelled at the success of this brand, and wondered why – and how – this particular product had become such a desirable thing for a fourteen-year-old. It turns out that this iced coffee drink started as an idea in a local manager's mind back in 1993, when Starbucks had just 300 stores. Dina Campion was a twenty-year-old employee who managed Southern California's ten stores.

She recalls, 'It was the summer of 1993, and Los Angeles is very hot in the summer. We noticed there were some smaller coffee shops that did some sort of blended coffee beverage. A couple of store managers and I felt there was a huge opportunity for Starbucks.'

Campion contacted one of her former California store managers, who had recently relocated to Seattle to work on the operations team at Starbucks' headquarters. They got the go-ahead to make their case with a test at a single store in Los Angeles' San Fernando Valley. Once that proved promising, they installed test sites at their busiest locations, and eventually in all of Campion's stores. The company soon acquired a small Boston chain called The Coffee Connection, which had perfected an iced blended drink called a frappuccino.

Over a five-month period, Starbucks developed store designs and blueprints for all of its 500-plus stores, and trained staff in all twenty-three of its markets. In the first summer of rollout, sales went from 100,000 to almost a million per week, as it proved just as popular in cold climate markets as it did in California. Frappuccinos ended up representing more than ten per cent of all revenues for the group. It later collaborated with PepsiCo to bottle the Frappuccino and its variants, and this product category now represents $2 billion in revenues for Starbucks globally.

This simple story illustrates the depth of cross-boundary thinking that needed to occur for the product to hit the shelves, expand across all stores, and then morph into a bottled product. It's unlikely you're in a consumer products business, but social goals demand solutions across boundaries more than ever before. Doctors have to work with community members to prevent spiralling chronic diseases. Prison operators have to work with educators to keep people from returning to jail. Infrastructure developers must work with governments to get permissions and financing deals. And those who genuinely turn the impossible into the possible can do this at scale, like Starbucks. They find ways to help ten people, not one, or a million, not a thousand.

To do any of these things, you need tools and methods that allow you to get an idea from one person's head (or a few people's) into the minds and hearts of many. What was a seed idea in Dina Campion's head back in 1993 is now present in my niece's mind a quarter of a century later, and in the minds of millions of others, too. Starbucks turned something *implicit* (something someone just knows, or feels) into something *explicit* (stuff that can be touched, seen, described, documented, drawn or explained).

You may not be in the iced coffee business (in fact, if you're reading this book, you almost certainly won't be!), but you share the same objectives, detailed in the chapters of this book:

- Reorienting your **purpose.**
- Changing or extending your **role.**
- Growing your **scale or reach.**
- Establishing new **goals.**
- Resetting your **values.**
- Trialling new **innovations.**
- Prioritising a new **initiative.**
- Testing new **partners.**
- Growing your **profile.**

Looking at the list above, how many have been on your agenda, or your organisation's agenda, just in the past twelve months? I would predict at least three or four, if not more. Wouldn't it be great if you knew you could bring your ideas to life, with a minimum of friction and stalling, and a maximum of energy and rapid melding? You can if you consider yourself the pilot, and others in your organisation the passengers.

In this final chapter, I'll show you how to win the hearts and minds of your target audience as you go, and, even more importantly, how to ensure that the ideas you choose to scale are your absolute best. In order to do that, I need to first address two common misconceptions.

Two common misconceptions about scaling ideas

In my experience of working with hundreds of groups and thousands of people over twenty years, I've noticed that the best organisations have pilots who can rapidly scale their organisation's best ideas by solving two misconceptions, or problems, that are common in public value organisations:

1. IF AN IDEA IS GOOD ENOUGH, PEOPLE WILL ACCEPT IT

Some executives honestly believe that a great product will speak for itself. They design and build the product, and then set up an ecommerce website. But the customers don't arrive. It doesn't matter how good the idea is; if it doesn't win the hearts and minds of its target audience, it's worthless. In the following section I'll show you, step by step, how to secure the success of your best ideas by ensuring they captivate the hearts and minds of your customers or beneficiaries.

2. IT'S TOO HARD TO HAVE THE HARD CONVERSATIONS

This misconception exists where an organisation's culture is fundamentally avoidant. This means that when opposition arises, as it must, people duck for cover. Or, even more perniciously, the opposition is never voiced! Later on, I'll reveal what the four main avoidance tendencies are, and how to reframe them to avoid common biases.

Ultimately, what you want are the highest quality ideas, built up over time by the right people, exercising the highest quality thought and debate. In order to do that, you need to solve both of the problems I've just outlined. The first problem can be solved via three-dimensional thinking, and the second can be solved by reframing common biases. These solutions are discussed in detail in the following sections.

Using 3D thinking to germinate your best ideas

You've no doubt experienced a situation where you have that seemingly magical combination of the right people, at the right time, taking an implicit idea and successfully making it explicit. I call this 3D thinking because you (or someone else) are, like a pilot, managing three dimensions simultaneously. Each of the three diagrams below shows a 'winning hearts' and 'winning minds' approach as a double-axis chart, moving from the lower left (a possibility in the mind of one person, or a few) to the upper right (a reality that is actionable by a large number of people).

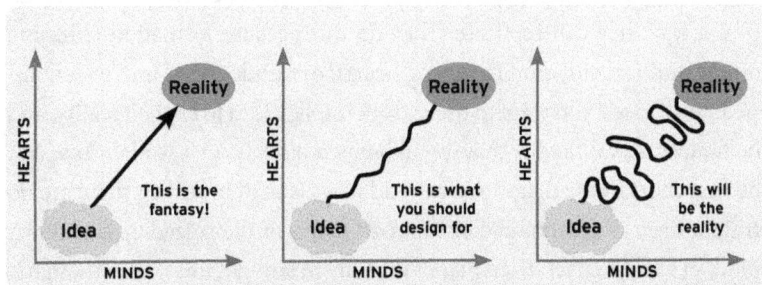

The first dimension is time (the diagonal). All collective ideas that are brought to life take time; they're far from instantaneous. The speed with which that happens depends largely on how the other two dimensions are handled. That is, winning people's hearts and minds. In Starbucks' case, the time dimension took a year from conception to launch.

The winning of minds is the second dimension (x-axis). This is the formation of the idea – from bare concept, often with many unresolved issues, to something that is realisable. This takes a seed – a germ of something that may have value – to something with some firm boundaries, and, finally, a practical product that can be executed. For Starbucks this was product testing, first internally, and then on customers to gauge uptake.

The third dimension (y-axis), winning hearts, is transmission. This means getting the idea from one person's mind (or the minds of a small group) into the minds of everyone involved. At Starbucks, this occurred hierarchically. Upwards at first, from Dina Campion to head office, but then outwards through training channels.

Many of the products you buy that are scaled for mass consumption are created by 3D thinking, including the aforementioned Starbucks Frappuccino. But equally, all social innovators use 3D thinking to germinate their best ideas. Unfortunately, not all of them succeed.

Organisations that get ideas from few to many, from concept to reality, do so in a way they can replicate. They do this because formation (winning minds) and transmission (winning hearts) are understood and well managed. In all cases, you want to move from implicit idea to explicit reality, and the fantasy we all hold is that it will happen quickly, in a straight line (see the first chart in the diagram). The bad news is that, in reality, there are no straight lines. Think about coastlines on maps, or the jagged up and down spikes of a share chart. Even planes don't fly in straight lines, even though it feels like they do! The good news is that you can realistically aim for *waves* that move successively upwards (see the second chart in the diagram).

What happens is that you develop the idea a bit (move across), then socialise it (move up). Rinse and repeat. The vertical movement is when you bring people together with the task of *improving the idea*. The horizontal movement is when your task is to *engage people with a (partially) formed idea.* Think again about how Starbucks did each of these with the Frappuccino. It rolled it out across multiple locations, in waves, and as the concept matured, in waves. Even this is an oversimplification of reality, though, as these three dimensions don't occur as separately as this – they mostly occur together. Furthermore, they're dependent on each other. Early stage transmission is best when the idea is still developing, while later stage transmission works best with mature ideas.

In my experience, it's common for formation and transmission to be uncoordinated and even invisible to each other. Consider for a moment that formation is often the domain of technical specialists, engineers, scientists, research and development specialists, and lawyers. In contrast, transmission is often in the wheelhouse of marketers, change managers, organisational development staff and strategic communications experts. Consequently, what usually happens is something that looks like the third chart in the diagram – the proverbial 'two steps forward, one step back' rate of progress.

The transmission gives rise to an important question that wasn't considered, and therefore sets the formation back. Or formation flags because hypotheses aren't sound, or can't be tested quickly, or at all. In any case, I advise my clients to not become discouraged, as this is part of the process. So, can we *design formation and transmission* to minimise the stalling and back-tracking? I'm glad you asked. From having led thousands of 3D group discussions, I've come to the view that there are some simple secrets that will enable you to ripple your ideas outwards to more people, while also testing your ideas.

The solution is to think of each dimension as being made up of three parts.

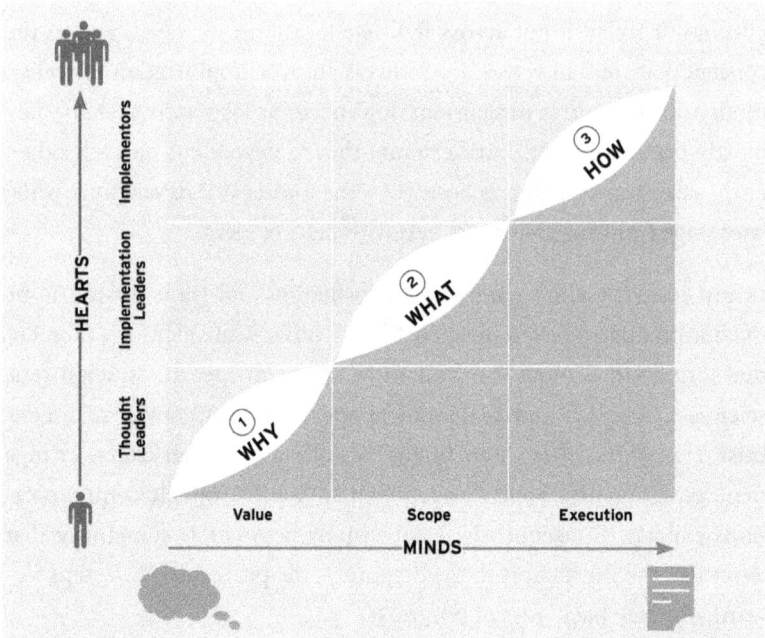

For the winning of hearts, it's helpful to think of the people you're piloting as ripples in a pond. Initially, at the possibility (or 'why') stage, it's necessary to work only with thought leaders. These are the people who are capable of *unlocking the true value* of the seed of an idea. They can, in a highly informed way, discuss:

- What's the result or outcome we're all seeking? Who has an interest in this?

- What is the germ of the idea? What methods, interventions and activities are required to develop it?

- How big is the initial and potential future impact of this idea?

- Who can lead, enlist support, participate and advocate? Whose support *must* we have?

- What resources are needed to develop this? What are *all* the resources that could be brought in? How could these be combined, or used more flexibly?

Once the idea survives these interrogations, a wider group of people – whom I refer to as implementation leaders – can be enlisted. These are pragmatists, probably drawn from the operational leadership levels of your organisation, and may also include specialists in people, technology, marketing and customer connection. Their job is to test the *scope* of the idea by asking 'what' questions:

- What does a working, but minimal, prototype of the idea look like?

- What evidence exists that the proposal will lead to the desired outcome?

- What tolerances does the prototype have to fall within (human, financial, organisational, reputational, political)?

- What sort of people should participate and to what degree? Whose support is essential?

- What are the obvious risks of this idea not working? If the idea *does* work, what are the risks to the business?

- What are the early users' experiences, and how can we amplify those that are positive?

- What variations occurred or could occur? Are these acceptable?

- What early results are scalable? How big could we make this?

Then, once the idea is deemed to survive this reality-testing phase, it can be put in the hands of implementers. The main imperative here is not to ask questions, but to *educate regarding execution*. Questions will of course arise, and must be answered, but the main educational focus is to engage people in the following 'how' questions:

- How will this improve key organisational metrics? What will happen if we don't do this?

- In detail, how do we roll out the idea in a practical sense, including potential dilemmas and problems to be solved, and changes required?

- How do we get the right people involved in leading, delivering and supporting the idea? (You should also take into account the personal involvement of people in the group.)

- How and where do we phase the rollout?

- How immediate or urgent is this, and what are our timelines or deadlines?

This final phase can be done not just in person, but by any means of large-scale education and behavioural change available to your organisation, including webinars, video-conferencing, online learning, and so on. The movement from internal to external, from intuitive to explicit, from few to many, from idea to reality, requires careful piloting.

So why doesn't this happen automatically, easily, quickly? Why does a collaborative idea sometimes start out well, but then, instead of coming to life, withers on the vine? What about where people are well intentioned but simply too busy carrying out 'business as usual' tasks? Or where they're defensive, protecting turf, maintaining silos and engaging in border skirmishes? Or where you can't even get to those stages, because there's just too much noise to generate the right ideas, or judge the best ideas? Or, perhaps collaborative work grinds to a halt because of complexity (incompatible goals, changing environments, too many moving parts, and so on). In short, is there a perception that it's simply too difficult to have the hard conversations? If so, you need to question whether certain biases are at play, and reframe those biases in a constructive way.

Reframing common biases that limit ideation

The best 'ideas teams' also recognise biases that affect group thinking, and can easily reframe their approach to eliminate these. The clearest example of four common biases of thinking was in a project I once worked on with a regulator. They had recently engaged another consulting firm to determine their desired culture and, not surprisingly, the organisation of 400+ people put forward cultural ideals such as 'proactivity', 'collaboration', 'sound judgement' and 'trust'. These all centred on constructive behaviours, which, if present, would enable them to thrive in their dynamic, highly contentious environment, where multiple interests would need to be balanced. So far, so good.

But then, the consultancy measured the current culture within this organisation. The good news was that it was capable of good judgement – this was an organisation bristling with PhDs. But there was low trust, and almost no collaboration. And proactivity was held down by routine risk assessments and advisory panels. The single word the consultants used to describe the culture of this organisation was 'avoidant'.

This term refers to an unwillingness to communicate, but, more specifically, to an unwillingness to communicate *when it's not easy to do so*. That is, when there's disputed territory, divergent objectives, or incompatible personality styles. In other words, people became unwilling to communicate so as to avoid conflict. In the case of this organisation, it was simply incapable of what I'd call high-quality thought. Its avoidance made it susceptible to four faults when it came to thinking in groups:

1. It placed too much credence on authority.

2. People didn't raise an issue when they saw it; they remained silent.

3. It explored complex issues insufficiently and failed to see how elements are connected.

4. It took positions too early, as expediency measures, and those who didn't agree were seen as 'unconstructive' and even locked out of discussions.

You might look at this and say, 'Well, this is pretty normal human behaviour. I see it all the time in my own organisation. Why is this a problem?' In this case, the regulator's avoidance meant that it overlooked a substantial risk to the sector it was regulating. It has since taken many years to reduce the harm, at a cost of tens of millions of dollars. Many affected businesses and organisations have had to take on substantial debt to pay for the clean-up and also to prevent future occurrences, and stakeholders are still paying it off today.

Conscious and deliberate piloting is required for new ideas to go from a vague conception in someone's mind to an executable idea that turns the impossible into the possible. Be as conscious and deliberate as you can be in both the winning of hearts and minds, and also the reframing of your conversations so as to eliminate or overcome common biases.

1

Confirmation Bias

This is the tendency to seek out, interpret and remember information that confirms a group's or organisation's pre-existing beliefs.

Reframe by asking:
- What's the evidence for X?
- Does X happen in all cases?
- What other explanations are there for X?
- How could we achieve X without compromising Y?

2

Authority Bias

This is not groupthink (the practice of thinking or making decisions as a group, typically resulting in unchallenged, poor-quality decision making), but leadthink. It shows up as false reasoning that says, 'As long as the leaders get it, it'll make sense to everyone else.' No, it won't. In fact, you'll get your best results when you actively question those in authority.

Reframe authority bias by asking:
- Is the person in charge always right?
  How should we best interpret their guidance?
- What are our sacred cows? Let's name them.
- Why are we not willing to challenge the fundholder or policymaker?

3

Premature Understanding

This is a hallmark of some individuals and teams, who pride themselves on rapid insigh and a solution-focused approach. Naturally, they want to get a result quickly. Who can blame them? The problem I observe is that often, they stop asking 'why' too early and hence focus on the wrong issues, or are railroaded into 'quick' decisions before root causes have been identified, or alternative courses of action properly evaluated.

To reframe premature understanding, ask:
- What don't we yet understand about this?
- What alternatives are available to us, apart from X?

4

Untruthfulness

This bias isn't outright lying - it's a sin of omission. This occurs when people feel psychologically threatened by speaking openly.

What needs to be asked is:
- Who's not saying something?
- Who's not listening?
- What are the benefits of not listening?
- What are the threats to speaking openly around here?

Frequently asked questions

There are three questions that my clients routinely ask me about how to facilitate discussions that elegantly take an idea from possibility to potential.

1. **Who should be involved if we want the highest quality ideas?**
   There is a myth that the best contributors to big ideas are those who can reach agreement quickly. These might be your *easiest* contributors, but I believe these are not your *best* contributors. What flies against convention, and comfort, is that your best contributors will include so-called 'difficult' people.

   But how can 'difficult people' be the 'right people' – those who bring about the highest quality thought and decision making? When I am leading collaborative ideas development, I meet three types of 'difficult people':

   - Those with *power* who are accustomed to cooperation through authority (for example, senior people who are used to people listening to their dictums without question).

   - Those *guarding territory* (for example, people who are protective of a philosophy, a product, or a team).

   - Those who are *argumentative* (for example, those who enjoy taking contrarian positions, almost as a sport).

   Each of these people *may* act as a saboteur if they are included in discussions, but they almost certainly *will* act as a saboteur if they are *not* included! Here are three guidelines to ensure their contribution is helpful rather than a hindrance:

   - Follow the dinner party rule. When I want to invite a difficult person for dinner, I don't invite them on their own. I don't invite several of them. I invite one or two, among a larger group. This way, the group norms are set by the majority, not the minority. In other words, don't let them dominate.

- Pre-frame, pre-frame, pre-frame. Don't jump straight into the discussion. Introduce the concept by talking about the bigger vision, the outcomes sought, and instances of past success. Limit their inputs by putting parameters around what you expect them to comment on. In other words, don't allow them total freedom of expression. And finally, enforce this: 'We agreed at the start that we wouldn't critique the idea, but we're here to map out as many benefits as possible.'

- Listen and acknowledge. Turn the difficult remarks into constructive feedback and useable material by enforcing the following: 'Remembering that we're being future-focused here, can you turn your complaint about past practices into positive guidance for us for the future?'

2. **How do I deal with people who are not open-minded and have already made up their minds?**

Sometimes individuals, or parts of groups, get to a 'no' position and it seems there's no budging them. In such cases, it's helpful to get inside the 'no' of decision making by facilitating a decision-making process that strengthens the group. The techniques of Deep Democracy, used in global peace and trade negotiations, are particularly useful here. One such technique masterfully avoids majority democracy (straightforward voting on a resolution) as it marginalises the 'no' voters. Instead, it's best to ask: 'Who supports the proposal in its current form?' Make it clear that it's safe to say 'no', so you can identify those with a concern. Next, hear them out. Log all the reasons. Then ask them: 'What do you need in order to go along with the group's decision?' In my experience, this process strengthens both the quality of the proposal, *and* the group. For those who are still unsupportive, simply state: 'We've worked on a proposal which the large majority supports and, on this occasion, you are outvoted.'

In summary, when you want to reframe position-taking, you should ask:

- What are the reasons why you can't support this?
- What would have to change for you to agree?

3. **How long should we take to get to a workable idea?**

Not as long as you think. I often remind my clients that perfection is the enemy of success, and that speed is utterly vital. You can often get to an eighty per cent workable idea using twenty per cent of your available time and effort. The diagram here shows this phenomenon visually, where trying to be perfect simply results in huge blocks of inefficiency.

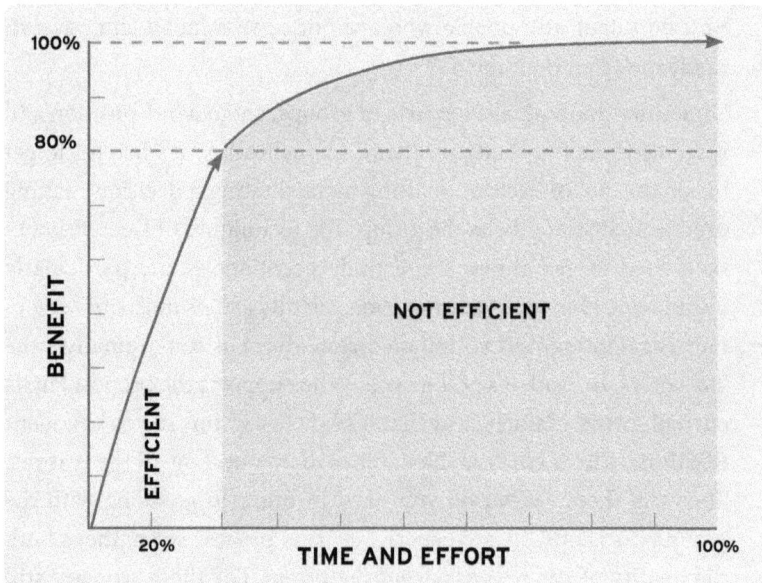

ACTION TO TAKE

This final chapter doesn't contain practical actions but, rather, guidance for you in leading complex or challenging discussions to make the impossible possible. Here are some key points to remember:

- Not every nail needs a hammer. Consult when you need to, not when others want you to.

- Make the complex as simple as possible, but not simpler.

- Learn from lean start-ups. Be satisfied with being eighty per cent right about the future.

- Be the leader everyone's looking at when it appears that nobody's in charge.

- Not all contributions are equal. Create a meritocracy of ideas.

- Consensus is overrated. Constructive disagreement is, in my experience, more important than agreement.

The true secret to making the impossible possible

Congratulations – you've made it to the end, and digested two vital rules of public value:

Rule 1: Know what your everyday impact should be.

Rule 2: Create everyday impact, every day.

In addition to digesting these two vital rules, I congratulate you in advance for having brave conversations with your people, whether it's about:

1. Your purpose, role, goals, values or scale (rule number one).

2. Taking ownership of results, where your efforts should be focused, how you innovate to make sure you're ahead of change requirements, how you leverage your customers, how you form partnerships with complementary organisations, and how you truly hold up a mirror to yourselves and build a profile around what you see (rule number two).

If you work on just one of these, you will notice a difference. And, just pick one to start with. Of course, if you work on all of them, you will notice a transformative change.

You can sense a 'but' coming, though, can't you?

Rule #3

In these final words, I'm here to tell you that neither of these rules, or any of the questions listed within the 'Action to Take' summaries of each chapter, will really enable you to make the impossible possible, unless you're capable of a third rule.

Rule number three is radical honesty.

Only radical honesty can overcome mediocrity, which is a subtle but insidious infection inside some non-profits and government agencies.

Radical honesty is the difference between having an intellectual understanding of the two rules, and a deep practical, visceral and emotional understanding of them. Sometimes, I work with clients who say, 'Andrew, we get it. We're doing our best, but we simply can't achieve what we want.'

On those occasions, I point out that perhaps they do know the right things to do, but there are deeper blockages that prevent them from shifting to a twenty-first century investor impact model. I usually diagnose one or more of five barriers which will cause catastrophic failure of any new idea, direction or venture:

1. **Doubt**. You (or others) fundamentally doubt your vision, doubt that it's necessary, or doubt that you have people good enough to be part of a new world.

2. **Sacred cows**. You have entrenched ideas about what must happen, who your customers must be, or how you must go about doing your work.

3. **Distrust**. You don't believe your colleagues' motives, others' commitment to follow through, or that others are as competent or capable as you are.

4. **Power**. Either nobody feels like they've got authority, or one person does and they dominate. Sometimes, those who have the authority are reluctant to use it.

5. **Politics**. You're burdened by past disagreements and 'water under the bridge', which cast conscious and unconscious shadows over any

new idea. This sometimes results in 'owing' allegiance to someone's ideas, even when that's not merited.

When one or more of these exist, you will find that you just can't get an intellectual engine room started and revved up, one that is going to deliver your most inspiring and realisable ideas, backed up by the best analysis and conceptualisation. You'll find that even though you start to have some of the conversations that this book encourages, you end up in a state of malaise and ordinariness. So, you stop doing it.

How can you smash through doubt, sacred cows, distrust, power and politics?

How do I encourage my clients to 'do' radical honesty?

I advocate three vows.

1. REJECT ORDINARINESS

Jeff Bezos, in the early days of Amazon, used Tuesdays and Thursdays as his quiet days, avoiding meetings and doing his own research instead. He would go shopping in traditional malls to see how merchandise was laid out. And he'd spend a lot of time exploring Amazon's own website, getting to know what was well built and what was flawed. He was searching for the non-ordinary. Back in 2000, he said, 'I only have a couple of roles. One is to make sure that people know that things that seem impossible often aren't. I'm well suited for that, knowing that everything we've done at Amazon seemed impossible at the time.'

So, the first thing you can do is open your eyes, ears and mind to noticing the non-ordinary. Think actively about what's not possible.

2. REJECT AVOIDANCE

I believe that avoidance (or, more accurately, not saying what you think and feel) is a major source of both occupational stress (for individuals) and poor performance (for organisations). Avoidant cultures are those that are fearful and stigmatised, where people get stuck in normative thinking ('This is what we've always done' or 'This is what everyone else does'). This keeps people inside the box and ensures they won't raise ideas in future.

The second thing you can do, therefore, is exercise the muscles of bluntness, forthrightness and directness. I'm not for a moment saying that you should be confrontational, aggressive or hurtful towards others. Rather, find ways to maintain rapport with others, but still put your views across clearly, in a way that meets your interests and theirs.

3. REJECT DISHONESTY

Look at the list of four biases on page 201 and ask yourself if any apply to your organisation. If they do, find people who are likely to at least partially understand your views and seek to have an honest conversation with them. Explicitly link one of the barriers to one of the elements of this book. For instance, start a conversation by saying things like:

- 'I'm concerned we can't have a meaningful discussion about scale, because we've got some **sacred cows** about how unique our service model is. I'd like us to question that.'

- 'It bothers me that when we talk about how we could build our profile, we limit ourselves with some basic **doubts** about how good we are. I think we should open up a discussion and give ourselves permission to be shamefully immodest about our achievements.'

- 'I'm suspicious that the reason we don't set and achieve goals is because nobody is stepping up to take **power** and control. I'd like an honest conversation about how we can do that better.'

Whatever the issue may be, name it and claim it.

Then, use the techniques outlined in this book to have frank (and occasionally difficult) conversations. When people do this, the feedback I routinely get is, 'We've never spoken like this to each other before!' and 'We've had breakthroughs I've only dreamed about.'

When you do this, you will re-energise and re-focus yourself, and your people. And it's with that energy and focus that you can make the impossible possible, even if it's only in small ways at first. With energy and focus, you can start to achieve visibility, growth and sustainability.

It doesn't end here

I find getting to the end of a book like this a little anti-climactic. Going back to the grind of everyday life after reading an inspirational book is a let-down. So if you're feeling that way, what could you do about it, to keep the fire alive? It's easy. Pass the book on. Talk to people about it. Recommend they read the dog-eared pages you've marked. If you don't want to hand your copy on, just contact me (see below) and I'll happily send your team members or colleagues additional copies with my compliments (in exchange for you telling me what you liked in the book, or what was most helpful to you!).

If you feel you need help with any of the ideas, exercises or discussions this book proposes, including breaking down the five barriers, don't hesitate to get in touch with me at http://workwell.com.au or drop me an email at ah@workwell.com.au. I'm always happy to talk.

For me, it's always an honour to work with people like you, who are striving to make the world a better place, now and for future generations.

Whether or not we ever meet in person, here's to making the impossible possible.

Andrew

Andrew Hollo

About the author

Andrew Hollo is best known for aligning diverse interests quickly and easily and synthesising the complex into workable strategies, so that his clients outperform their own expectations. He works with all types and sizes of public value organisations: from boutique think tanks of a half dozen people, to enormous government behemoths with tens of thousands of staff and budgets of tens of billions of dollars.

Andrew can be reached at ah@workwell.com.au.

Acknowledgements

First and foremost, I acknowledge my numerous clients. If you are one of them, you already know how you are changing the lives of the people whom your services, your policies and your efforts benefit. If I'm being truthful, the authoring of this book is only half mine. The other half belongs to my clients with whom I've been privileged to share the many 'aha moments' that form every chapter of this book. I hope the synthesis of these hundreds of 'aha' moments in the form of a book adds just a little to your abilities and confidence to do your best work. In particular, and I won't name the numerous people who did so, I want to thank all of my clients who gave me honest and undiluted feedback on the book they wanted to read (or want their staff to read). I hope the book you now have before you is it.

I also thank those who have inspired and supported me to be more than a consultant, but a writer too. First, profound gratitude to Alan Weiss, the pioneer of the notion that the most effective consultants should also be thought leaders. This book wouldn't have emerged so quickly if it wasn't for Jacqui Pretty, founder of Grammar Factory, who has built a streamlined process that shepherded my book from a messy draft into the words you're reading now, Michelle Hammond, whose rigorous editing made me feel like I was back at school and was handed back work with many red pen corrections and suggestions through it, and Charlotte Gelin, designer of the wonderful cover and internals, who put up with my changing my mind at least ten times before we got everything right. Also, very big thanks to Sharon Holmes, who designed all of the diagrams in the book (and in my consulting work for the past two years). Your ability to mind-read what I'm trying to convey, and stay calm and focused throughout this process, has been wonderful.

My warmest gratitude of all goes to Kate Challis, my insightful, discerning, clever and beautiful wife. She sternly sent me off to Bali for a week to write the first draft of this book – and told me to keep going when all I wanted to do was stop writing and just work on what seemed much easier, that is, helping to solve my clients' strategic problems. Over late night negronis, she kept prodding and re-testing my ideas. I'd awaken in the morning, clear about how those ideas could be combined, edited or altered and thereby made immeasurably better. And, last, she did what all great partners do: Believe in me, even when I didn't believe in myself, often with just a glance, or a smile.

Impact Scorecard

Discover your organisation's impact and increase your ability to be a visionary leader

Your value as a leader is directly related to your ability to articulate your organisation's value - and to align it.

You've read the book – so it's a good idea to see where you stand. Do the Workwell Impact Scorecard and get feedback on how you can create strategy that is better:

Owned by your leaders
Believed in by your people and customers
Invested in by funders and partners

Answer 33 questions and get your Impact Scorecard. It's free of charge, with no strings attached, and takes less than 15 minutes.

The Impact Scorecard will measure you against all 11 elements in this book:

Purpose	Role	Scale	Goals	Values	Leverage

Partner	Focus	Future Proof	Results	Profile

You'll get an immediately downloadable report, with instantly implementable advice – and practical questions to put to your team, customers or partners.

Discover Your Organisation's Impact
visit: https://workwell.com.au/impact-scorecard/

workwell.

Index

www.ingramcontent.com/pod-product-compliance
Lightning Source LLC
Chambersburg PA
CBHW020834210326
41598CB00019B/1894